There is nothing which brings a period to life quite as much as a biographical sketch, and the period of the Reformation is especially rich in memorable characters. Christopher Catherwood's fluent style brings out the broad sweep of a spiritual movement which transcended national barriers and has left a permanent mark on Europe and in the wider world. He shows how five men of very different personality and outlook could all be caught up in the same experience of a life transformed by the power of God. The portraits are painted "warts and all" but the message is clear - God can and does use the weak and imperfect things of this world to proclaim his message of salvation in Christ to all who believe. This book will bring that truth home to a new generation of readers, and I commend it warmly.

Gerald Bray
Beeson Divinity School
Birmingham, Alabama

Christopher Catherwood tells t̲_____̲ve Reformation leaders. His work is ṉ_____ ̲ᵤ honesty, for he does not look away from their flaws. But Catherwood also shows how their lives were touched by greatness from God, for He must be the ultimate explanation for the reformers' accomplishments. This book reminds the modern reader that believers in the gospel have had their backs to the wall before. We are surrounded by a great cloud of witnesses, like the reformers, whose lives prove that the challenge can be met. Finally, Catherwood does not merely re-tell familiar facts. He opens up their meaning and relevance, so that one is drawn into the drama with effortless fascination. As I read, I was constantly making connections with our present-day situation. It was a privilege to read this book, and it is a delight to recommend it.

Ray Ortlund, Jr.
Senior Minister, First Presbyterian Church,
Augusta, Georgia

The Reformation upheaval of the 16th century had national, cultural, social and political aspects as well as opening a new era on the theological, ecclesiastical and religious fronts, and historians, like theologians, find it endlessly interesting. Here Christopher Catherwood, a writer abreast of ongoing historical study of the period and aware of the spiritual issues hanging on the chain of events, tracks five major players from the cradle to the grave: Luther, Zwingli, Calvin, Cranmer, Knox. Each in his way was a watershed figure, and Catherwood's vivid profiling of them will help to keep their memory green.

J I Packer
Regent College, Vancouver

This is a vigorous insider's account of five churchmen and theologians prominent in the movement that transformed the face of Christendom. The author emphasises especially the political dimension of the Reformation, and with it the emancipation of lay people. He corrects caricatures, without portraying plaster saints. This is a religious biography with a message for today, lest we forget.

David Wright
New College, Edinburgh

Five Leading Reformers

Christopher Catherwood

Christian Focus

ISBN 1 85792 507 6

Published in 2000
by
Christian Focus Publications,
Geanies House, Fearn, Ross-shire,
IV20 1TW, Great Britain.

Cover design by Owen Daily

Contents

Introduction

The Reformation, which many historians regard as beginning in 1517, when a hitherto obscure German monk nailed 95 theological propositions, or 'theses', to a door of a church in Wittenberg, has continued to be one of the most controversial events in the history of the world. The fact that today we have Protestant as well as Roman Catholic and Orthodox churches is living witness to those momentous times. Some view it as a triumph, others as a tragedy;[1] no one can be indifferent. We live in the world that the Reformation has made.

History, though, is never that simple. In order to understand the past effectively, we must first examine the methods through which we can best comprehend what happened and why.

Methodological Preliminary

Historians used to believe that it was possible to be completely objective, and that one could give an entirely objective, scientific picture of the past. Historians both Reformed and Catholic have in recent books[2] argued that this is simply impossible: *everyone* has a bias of some kind or another, and history writing, rather than being a contest between objective[3] and subjective, is really between those who are honest in revealing their personal view,[4] so that you can judge their work accordingly, and those who delude themselves into thinking they have suppressed it.

Complete objectivity is, therefore, surely impossible

7

with the vast and ever-growing number of sources open to the historian; even the selection of what one picks to be included is frequently subjective.

However, all reputable historians do regard it as vital to be *honest*.[5] It is essential, if one discovers something inconvenient to one's own viewpoint, to include it in the text. This might mean that people reading your book will come to disagree with you – but that is a risk one has to take! For those of us who are both practising Christians and historians, honesty is especially important: indeed it is no less than a command of God![6]

Providential Views of History[7]

If I am to give my own viewpoint, or starting place, I can begin by saying that I am myself a Protestant, of a theologically conservative kind, with a world view predominantly in tune with that of the Reformers, and of John Calvin in particular. My ancestral tradition would be very sympathetic with John Knox and I attend a church in which Thomas Cranmer would have felt at home.[8]

Having said all that, I will aim in this book to be as fair as possible to all points of view. As we shall see, the great Reformers differed greatly with one another on several key issues, as well as with the Roman Catholic Church from which they had split.

I myself, for example, disagree with Calvin on the issue of baptism – despite being happy to call myself 'Reformed' in general, I would hold to a believer's baptism theology rather than the 'covenant baptism' doctrine to which Calvin held. This would put me in disagreement with all five of the subjects of this book. I hope, however, that will not put you off what follows!

Like all the five subjects though, I am a strong believer in God's present-day activity in history. Many of you may share this perspective. If you do, there are some important methodological preliminaries.

When we read the Bible, we read about the activities of God in history. Like the Reformers, many of us believe that God inspired the accounts there, so we can see his action, and sometimes his thought processes, at work.

Some biblical insights
However, we are now living in post-biblical times in which things are not always so clear cut. God has laid down for us eternal rules and principles. But we don't have the same detailed insights that the Apostles were privileged to have; for instance, Bible-believing Christians of all hues still disagree on the exact meaning of biblical teaching on church government. In the same way, we don't know what events in more recent history are beneficial for sure, and which are not. Most Protestants would, I imagine, hold that God was at work through the Reformers in the sixteenth century. But would those who believe deeply that we alone choose to be saved always regard Calvin as a good thing – or as a mistake? Likewise, would all Baptists hold Knox or Cranmer as heroes? Maybe – but maybe not.

Likewise, we should also remember from Scripture that God works providentially, through human beings.[9] We know that even Apostles like Peter and Paul disagreed.[10] Perhaps disagreements between Luther and Calvin, for instance, look less alarming in that light.

But this also means that in the same way that God used pagan rulers such as Pharaoh[11] or Cyrus[12] to benefit God's chosen people in Old Testament times, so too God can go on using secular things, events or peoples to his purposes. So when historians say that printing made a huge difference to the Reformation, or that economic/political/social discontent made people receptive to the Reformation message, they are not of necessity denying that God is at work behind the scenes. Non-Christian historians can give equally good insights into Reformation history and often do. Few people have understood the Puritans as well as the distinguished British historian, Christopher Hill, a Marxist non-Christian.

Whether or not, therefore, particular events are providential depends a lot on your point of view: whether or not Calvin interpreted the Bible correctly, or which view of church government or baptism is correct. Since, in this book, I am trying to be honest and open-minded between different viewpoints (despite my own declared prejudices), I deliberately therefore don't say whether or not God was behind a particular event, person, movement or doctrine. I do believe that God was powerfully at work in the extraordinary events of the sixteenth century, but in what way precisely, I leave you, the reader, to decide for yourself.

Protestant saints

Lastly, one of the ironies of history is that while Protestants deny the Catholic doctrine of specially meritorious individuals, or 'saints', we often canonise our own heroes and all but turn them into Protestant saints.

This is especially true if we agree with them. We try and cover up obnoxious personality traits because we admire the writing or doctrinal insights of a particular individual or group.

Yet we forget that they were both men of their times –

for example, Luther's anti-Semitism, Zwingli's resort to war with those who disagreed with him – as well as giants of the faith.

Similarly, we can act the other way around, rejecting a doctrine because we dislike the individual: many reject Calvin's interpretation of Scripture because of their strong antipathy to his personality.

My hope is that in reading this book, you will come to a more balanced view: 'I dislike X, but agree with him on Z', or 'I agree with X on A and B, but disagree with him on C and D.' Protestants may, after all, agree that the Bible is true, but it is the *Bible alone* (*sola scriptura*), not individual interpreters of it.

Final note

This is a work of *secondary* material, to use the language of history writing. I have not delved into the archives for *primary* material, but have read extensively the works of other historians, those who have laboured long with the original manuscripts. The primary work is therefore theirs, the distillation into one volume is mine. Likewise any mistakes are mine too. I trust therefore that you will go on to read more detailed works after reading this and, if so inspired, the original works of the subjects themselves.

References

1. Oliver R. Barclay, quoting David Watson, in *Evangelicalism in Britain 1935-1995: A Personal Sketch* (Leicester, 1997) p. 103.

2. See George Marsden, *The Soul of the American University* (New York and Oxford, 1994), esp. pp. 429-444, and also Adrian Hastings, *The Construction of Nationhood: Ethnicity, Religion and Nationalism* (Cambridge, 1997) p. 33. See also my article on the issue, 'Nationalism, Academia and Modernity: a Reply' in *Transformation*, vol.14, no. 4 (October/December 1997) pp.26-31.

3. For those who take the increasingly old-fashioned view that their personal views can be objectively suppressed by writing in 'scientific' style, see J. McManners, *The Oxford Illustrated History of Christianity* (Oxford and New York, 1990) pp. 1-18, esp. 4-5.

4. For an honest view approach, see for example Marsden, ibid., and Felipe Fernandez-Armesto and Derek Wilson in *Reformation: Christianity and the World 1500-2000* (London and New York, 1996) passim, henceforth abbreviated to FFA/DW.

5. I give this issue full discussion in *A Crash Course on Church History* (London, 1998) pp.2-5.

6. Deuteronomy 5:20.

7. Catherwood, *Crash Course*, pp. 8-9 for further discussion.

8. For a detailed look at the issue of self-identity and the historian, see C. Catherwood, *Why the Nations Rage* (London, 1997), pp. 3-23.

9. This should be obvious, but see Hebrews 11 for explicit confirmation.

10. Paul withstood Peter to his face: see Galatians 2:11-21.

11. Exodus 5: 21–10:20.

12. Ezra 1: 1-4.

1

Martin Luther

1415	Martyrdom of Czech Reformer Jan Hus
1467	birth of Erasmus of Rotterdam
1471	publication of Thomas à Kempis' book *The Imitation of Christ*
1483	birth of Martin Luther
1505	Luther's decision to become a monk
1513-18	Luther changes theology: exact timing disputed
1516	Erasmus publishes his Greek New Testament translation
1517	Luther nails his 95 theses to the Wittenberg door
1520	Luther composes three critically important pamphlets setting out his views, including salvation by faith alone: *sola fides*
1520	Pope condemns Luther
1521	Luther defends his views at the Diet of Worms and has to flee
1522	Luther's New Testament translation: in German not Latin
1525	Luther marries Katherine
1526	The Diet of Speyer: the Holy Roman Empire increasingly split so many secular rulers support Luther
1529	Luther's Catechisms
1530	The Confession of Augsburg summarises Protestant belief
1546	Luther dies after spending many years consolidating the new church

Some opening thoughts

As we saw, those of us on the Protestant side of the divide are used to thinking of the Reformation as beginning on October 1517, with Martin Luther, a hitherto obscure priest in a backwater part of Germany.

Historians now, however, argue that it might not be that simple. As with all historical debates, there is no consensus on exactly when the Reformation began, or how important it was if we consider the story of Christianity as a whole.

So if we are to understand Luther and his true importance, we need first of all to consider: what was the Reformation? Was it a clean break with the past? A staging post in a continuous saga of ongoing Reformation? Or part of a continuous process but a very major one, far bigger than any Reform before or since?

Purifying Holy Church

'God will purify Holy Church (sic) by awakening the spirit of the elect. This will lead to such an improvement in the Church of God and such a renewal in the lives of her holy pastors that at the mere thought of it my spirit exalteth in the Lord.'[1]

Some great Reformer? Luther himself? No, the quotation is actually from the fourteenth-century Catholic mystic, St. Catherine of Siena.

One school of historians argues that the Reformation, while important, was part of a process of continual change, reformation and renewal. Others hold to the traditional school: that what Luther began was the start of something completely new, changing the Church permanently.

So, to understand what I think is Luther's major achievement, we need to examine these two schools of thought, to understand more fully how this obscure Saxon monk, born far away from the great centres of Renaissance Italy, was able to make the difference that he did, with the consequences which are still very much with us today.

A continuing story?

The new school of thought is very much that the Reformation was not a 'divisive event', but a 'continuing story'.[2] As Felipe Fernandez-Armesto, a Catholic, and Derek Wilson, an Anglican Evangelical, put it in their book, *Reformation*: 'The Reformation looks like a stage in a long transformation of Christianity, a common project of Catholic, Protestant and Orthodox reformers', with the years since 1517 being 'an era of creative diversity, overarching unity and dynamic promise'.[3]

What Catholics have called 'continual Reformation', they call 'sporadic Reformation', because, as we can all agree, the Church is made up of human beings, with all our fallibility.

They continue:

What has been traditionally called 'the Reformation' was only the most violent of these jolts. Luther, Zwingli and Calvin or their Catholic counterparts, like Erasmus, Cisneros and Contarini, were arguing for some of the same ingredients of spiritual renewal which Bernard, Francis and Wycliffe had advocated.[4]

Consequently, if we accept the continuity argument,

then the Reformation ceases to be central in the sense that we see some events 'leading up' to it and others 'flowing from' it.... This does not mean that the Reformation, as traditionally understood, never happened or that its importance has been exaggerated: only that it did not happen as commonly supposed and that its importance has been wrongly assigned.[5]

In fact, for them Reformation is not only a continuous, but also a permanent thing, not a past event but something more important than that: it is 'still active and influential – indeed, powerfully reverberent – in the present'.[6]

Nor was what Luther did essentially new. 'Rather,' they argue, 'than a new departure in Church history, it was a growth out of long traditions, a form of age-old diversity.'[7]

This was because

The Reformation did not come as a torrent in a parched land. People responded to the challenging ideas of emancipated preachers and propagandists because they appeared to meet already perceived needs....The vehicle might have been thrust suddenly from second into fifth gear in the 1520s, but it was already moving.[8]

So, was Luther's importance exaggerated? This book is a biographical study, looking at five key individuals of the sixteenth century. But I think that we can see their importance if we re-examine the traditional view, and see that it has, perhaps, more life in it than new writers think.

Tradition revisited?

Since Eamon Duffy's recent seminal work on the pre-Reformation English church, *The Stripping of the Altars*, historians have recognised that the late medieval church was by no means as lifeless as traditional Protestant historiography has made out.

In part, this has been because we looked at the obvious horrors – such as the Borgias with their flagrant immorality – rather than at ordinary grass-roots religion, where popular traditional belief was much stronger.

Here, indeed, the fact that the church was very flexible to local demands meant that Reformation was, if anything, less likely to happen.[9] Religion was the mediator between ordinary people and God, and 'gave people a forum and a structure for their social life.'[10]

Much of this popular piety was very superstitious, with a major role being played by relics – one of the biggest collections of such objects being held by Luther's political overlord, the Elector of Saxony, Frederick the Wise.

But while grass-roots Christianity was strong, the medieval church was distinctly vulnerable.[11] It was very difficult to get impetus going *from within*, especially because the bureaucratic obstruction against internal reform remained massive. Nor was the medieval Papacy as powerful as it liked to think: it always depended on the collaboration of the local prince or king, especially in the area of ecclesiastical appointments to important posts.

One particular lay movement pointed towards internal *spiritual* reform. This was the *devotio moderna* of the Brethren of the Common Life.[12]

Birth of a Pivotal Figure

Martin Luther was born on 10 November 1483, in the town of Eisleben, in the Electorate of Saxony. His father, Hans Luther, was a copper miner by trade, and soon after Martin's birth, he, his wife Margarette, and Martin were on the move again, as Hans slowly climbed the social ladder.

Luther's upbringing was a stern one, something that more recent psychologists have emphasised.[13] On the other hand, it was probably typical of the rough, originally poor but socially mobile, family of the time, so perhaps not too much stress can be laid upon it. The main thing is that his childhood was not privileged in any way. Luther, who has been described as 'one of the pivotal figures of Western civilization',[14] came from an area where the main flowering of Renaissance civilisation was largely unknown, thereby making his achievement all the more remarkable.

The family moved to the Saxon town of Mansfeld, where Luther was educated at the local Latin school, Latin being, in those days, the key international language of scholarship. (This helped a great deal – someone writing in Hungary could be read in Sweden, England or Spain and fully understood in each place because all learned men wrote in the same language.)

Luther then spent a year in Magdeburg, at a school run by the Brethren of the Common Life, the forward-looking devotional group with which Erasmus had close links.[15] The best-known early exponent of this group was Thomas à Kempis (1380-1471), the author of the devotional classic, *The Imitation of Christ*. Saxony might have missed out on the glories of Renaissance Florence, but important, groundbreaking theology managed to find its way through.

Like many fathers from humble backgrounds, Hans

Luther had big ambitions for his clever son. He wanted him to be a lawyer. So in 1501, young Martin matriculated at the nearby University of Erfurt, which, while not internationally renowned like Paris, Oxford or Bologna, was regarded as one of northern Europe's most popular universities.

Here Luther did well. He became a skilled philosopher, studied the liberal arts, gaining his bachelor's degree on 29 September 1502, and his Master's degree on 7 January, coming second in his class. He looked well-set for legal success.

Luther the monk: salvation by penitential works

His father's fond ambitions were to be overthrown by a dramatically unexpected event. One sunny July day (2 July 1505) the young Luther was suddenly caught in a thunderstorm. St. Anne was the patron saint of miners such as Hans Luther, so Martin, when faced with what he thought might be sudden death from a lightning bolt, cried out, 'St. Anne help me! I will become a monk.'[16]

Luther's call to the spiritual life was not, then, a usual one. His psychology is difficult to interpret at this distance,[17] especially since the terminology that we use today was unknown then, quite apart from the fact that people will often interpret someone's psychological profile by whether they agree or disagree with someone's views.

Thankfully for historians, though, Luther wrote copiously on his own life and thought. About his rather abrupt decision to become a monk, he wrote in 1521 that 'not freely or desirously did I become a monk, but walled around with the terror and agony of sudden death, I vowed a constrained and necessary vow'.[18]

In other words, he became a monk from fear: fear of death and fear of the consequences of death. This was reinforced by the words of the Prior of the Augustinian Order which Luther joined: 'Not he that hath begun but he that endureth to the end shall be saved.'[19]

It was endurance that would save him, rather than anything else – or so he thought. The main thrust of medieval Christianity, the penitential cycle, was one based very strongly on works, things you did, to earn merit and thereby secure salvation. To a mind such as Luther's, with all his inner turmoil and doubts, this was the worst possible cure, since he could never be sure that, however hard he strove, he would finally get to heaven.

What made it more terrible for Luther was the idea that you could be damned for unconfessed sins that you did not know that you had committed, something with which he used to bother his superior, Staupitz.[20] Staupitz became so frustrated with Luther's endless quest to find *everything* to confess that at one stage he urged Luther to kill someone to have something really big to confess!

Then Luther became more despondent still, thinking, 'Have I been truly contrite in my confession? Or is my repentance motivated merely by fear?'[21] Thinking that he was not truly repentant enough, he began to wish that he 'had never been created a human being'.[22]

Staupitz's extraordinary way of dealing with Luther's ups and downs was to set Luther the task of giving a whole series of Bible lectures, which involved Luther in close study of the Scriptures.[23] Medieval theology was dominated by a series of debates between different schools of theology, one of the most famous philosophers being William of Occam, whose teachings were well-known to Luther.[24]

There is not space here to go into the precise details of nominalism and other medieval thought patterns, other than to say that Luther's agony was prolonged and neither the German mystic theologians nor the medieval nominalists proved to be of much help in Luther's agonising quest for assurance of salvation.

Although Luther's works are copious, not to mention works about Luther as well,[25] Luther's memory in his later years makes the *exact* dates of Luther's thought changes difficult to pinpoint. We can, however, know for sure when he lectured on various Biblical books, because the results were often published. His lectures on Psalms began on 16 August 1513, those on Galatians on 27 October.

But it was his lectures on Romans that were to change both Martin Luther and the world.

Up until then, Luther, for all his inner turmoil, had been a loyal son of the Catholic Church. This was despite Luther's trip to Rome itself, made in late 1510. He was appalled by the sheer stench of corruption and lax morality he saw there. As historians have made clear, though, many Catholics, like Erasmus, were horrified at the corruption too, but without ever leaving the Catholic Church.[26] Furthermore, some, like Cardinal Contarini, were independently advocating many of the doctrines that Luther was soon to make famous, such as justification by faith, and that in Rome itself![27]

Conversion of a future reformer

So what happened to Luther? When did it happen? It may seem odd, but historians are no longer sure exactly when Luther's conversion took place.[28] What we do know is that at some stage, probably between 1513 and 1518, Luther had what has now become called 'the Tower experience', named after the physical location, in a tower, where it took place. It was here that he probably began the experience that led to his conversion. At the beginning, Luther was a loyal Catholic. By the end he had turned not only his own world upside down but that of Western Christendom itself.[29]

Luther decisively rejected his past, scholasticism, and discovered the assurance of faith which he had been seeking for so long. We cannot do better than to look at it in his own words:[30]

I greatly longed to understand Paul's Epistle to the Romans and nothing stood in the way but that one expression, 'the justice of God', because I took it to mean that justice whereby God is just and deals justly in punishing the unjust. My situation was that, although an impeccable monk, I stood before God as a sinner troubled in conscience, and I had no confidence that my merit would assuage him. Therefore I did not love a just and angry God, but rather hated and murmured against him. Yet I clung to the dear Paul and had a great yearning to know what he meant.

Night and day I pondered until I saw the connection between the justice of God and the statement that 'the just shall live by his faith'. Then I grasped that the justice of God is that righteousness by which through grace and sheer mercy God justifies us through faith. Thereupon I felt myself to be reborn and to have gone through open doors into paradise. The whole of Scripture took on a new meaning and whereas before the 'justice of God' had filled me with hate, now it became to me inexpressibly sweet in greater love. This passage of Paul became to me a gate to heaven....

If you have a true faith that Christ is your Saviour, then at once you have a gracious God, for faith leads you in and opens up God's heart and will, that you should see pure grace and overflowing love. This it is to behold God in faith that you should look upon his fatherly, friendly heart, in which there is no anger nor ungraciousness. He who sees God as angry does not see him rightly but looks only on a curtain, as if a dark cloud had been drawn across his face.

I think that there is a very good case for saying that *this* is when the Reformation really began, when Luther finally realised that the 'righteous shall live by *faith*'. This was the true starting point, in terms of the core theology of the Reformation. Certainly, some Catholics, such as the Oratory of Divine Love, had come to similar conclusions via a different route.[31] But none of them did anything like as much as Luther was to do with the discovery. Indeed, one of them, the English Cardinal, Reginald Pole, was to end up an active persecutor of Protestants under his distant cousin, Queen Mary I, in the 1550s.

Revolutionary reformation
The theological importance of Luther's discovery of justification by faith cannot be overestimated. While historians argue over the causes of the Reformation, it was this doctrine, *sola fide*, that was the theological spark that ignited the fire (along with, as we shall see, the doctrine of scripture, *sola scriptura*).

Timothy George has aptly written:

Luther's doctrine of justification fell like a bombshell on the theological landscape of medieval Catholicism. It shattered the entire theology of merits and indeed the sacramental-penitential basis of the church itself.[32]

As Euan Cameron puts it, for Luther, justification by faith was 'the summary of Christian doctrine' and the 'sun which illuminates God's Holy Church.'[33]

I think this point is crucial because the Reformation was not just about reforming the church, it was something revolutionary. However much Contarini, Erasmus, Pole and others believed in reform, and, in Contarini's case, perhaps even justification by faith as well, none did so in the way in which Luther did. This is why Cameron is surely right to argue (a) that Luther did something new and (b) in a way which both liberated and involved *ordinary Christians*.

Protestants tend to emphasise the corruption of the old pre-Reformation Catholic Church. As we have seen, this might have been exaggerated if one considers grass-roots piety, as opposed to high-level corruption such as Alexander VI (the Borgia Pope) or the intensely warlike Pope Julius II, who was more a warrior than a spiritual leader. So Luther could have, as he did, complain against the abuses within the Church and, as Erasmus did, complain *without* leaving. However, Luther could hardly stay when the full logic of his views on justification by faith was worked out. Luther's view, whether new or not, was certain, when fully developed, to undermine the basic tenets of medieval Catholicism.[34] Many believers in the Middle Ages were sincerely devout people. But their beliefs were essentially works or merit orientated, and the basis of Catholicism at that time was that the church was the mediator of these acts of merit between God and ordinary Christians.

Cameron, like George, shows conclusively that in breaking this link, Luther, and his doctrine of justification by faith, fundamentally undermined the Church. As he writes, the common themes of the Reformation message justified, indeed required, a clean sweep of the institutions and practices of the old Church. By asserting its corporate monopoly of the 'means of grace' (sacramental absolution and penance, the mass, intercessions, indulgences and so on) the old Church had partly counterbalanced the resentment and criticism which its moral and practical shortcomings aroused. In the Reformation that equilibrium was destroyed, because reputable and persuasive figures convinced many people that their souls were really saved *without* the paraphernalia of the sacramental and penitential system.[35]

This meant, then, that, as Cameron continues,

the Church . . . had no excuse for its deficiencies: indeed its spiritual ministry, which had excused its other faults before, now itself became a blasphemy against Christ. A simple anticlerical attack on the morality and status of the clergy could never have been so destructive.

Furthermore, as Cameron goes on to conclude:

The Reformation destroyed the penitential cycle by the most subtle, roundabout means. Luther and his successors *re-examined the theology of salvation itself* (my italics), by appealing to biblical sources, than which nothing was better calculated to catch the mood of the age. . . . At every critical point they challenged, redefined, and rearranged the very building-blocks of medieval belief: sin, law, faith, justification, the Church, in explicit defiance not only of the 'Occamist School', but of a much broader medieval consensus.

Luther's theses v. Tetzel's jingle

That is why I believe that the Reformation, in effect, began *before* Luther discovered the now-famous abuses of Tetzel, the monk selling indulgences. This is because the effect of what Luther was saying was not just, 'I think indulgences are wrong', but 'indulgences are the symptom of a much more deeply rooted disease, the very nature of the understanding of salvation itself (my words, not Luther's)'. This is also why, although we classically start the Reformation on 31 October 1517 and the nailing by Luther of his 95 theses against Tetzel's actions, the *spiritual* origins of the Reformation must surely be dated earlier. (Is this an argument for an earlier date for the Tower experience? Perhaps – I am sure that it is a persuasive argument for a pre October 1517 date.)

This, therefore, is why Luther is important, and why *sola fidei* is seen as the heart of Reformation faith.

Several months before the 95 theses, in May 1517, Luther was already writing to a friend: 'My theology – which is St. Augustine's – is getting on, and is dominant in the university.'[36] This was the University of Wittenberg where he was now a professor of theology, having gained his doctorate in 1512. Characteristically, Luther went on to write:

> God has done it. Aristotle is going downhill and perhaps he will go all the way down to hell . . . . Nobody will go to hear a lecture unless the lecturer is teaching my theology – which is the theology of the Bible, of St. Augustine and of all true theologians of the Church.

As Luther concluded:

I am quite sure that the Church will never be reformed unless we get rid of canon law, scholastic theology, philosophy and logic as they are studied today, and put something else in their place.

Many historians have pointed out that Luther never originally set out to create a new Church.[37] What one can argue, though, is that once he did set out, a new Church became reasonably inevitable or increasingly likely. As other historians have demonstrated, people had been *talking* for a long time about the abuses within the Church.[38] Luther went one further and *did* something.

Furthermore, one can argue also that because Luther's *prime* starting point was *spiritual*, he had more impact. Timothy George is surely right, therefore, to say that

Luther's protest against the Roman Church was not primarily *moral* (my italics), as was that of Erasmus and other reformers [sic], but rather *theological* (my italics). God's grace was *God's* grace. It could not be bought, sold, or parcelled out in indulgences.[39]

So when Luther discovered that a man called Tetzel was travelling around northern Germany selling indulgences, he was outraged, because his own theology already told him that this was wrong.

In fact, Luther was, technically speaking, wrong in his precise condemnation of what Tetzel was actually doing,[40] not that this mattered at all in terms of Luther's theological appraisal of Tetzel's actions.

Luther condemned Tetzel for trying to get money for Pope Cleo X, of the famous Florentine Medici family, to build the new Cathedral of St. Peter in Rome. Technically this was incorrect. The actual situation was that the youthful Albert of Brandenburg (brother of the Elector of Brandenburg), having become Archbishop of Magdeburg while still a child, had had to borrow huge sums of money from the Imperial bankers, the Fuggers, to pay the Pope to get a dispensation to become Archbishop of Mainz as well. (This was one of the three Archbishoprics which also made the holder one of the seven Electors who chose the holy Roman Emperor, and therefore had great political as well as ecclesiastical importance.) Albert needed to repay his vast debts, and the Pope agreed that this could be done through selling indulgences. So the Pope *would* benefit financially, but *indirectly* since the actual proceeds from the sale would go to Albert first.

Tetzel's jingle that 'the moment the money tinkles in the collection box, a soul flies out of purgatory'[41] outraged Luther. An indulgence meant that if you paid some money to the collector, the Pope would exercise his power in removing a poor soul from Purgatory, the place in which, according to the Catholic Church, souls had to wait, until they were sufficiently meritorious, before getting to heaven (Protestants believe that since the Bible does not mention such a place, it does not exist. Luther eventually taught that too, though, as we shall see, not straight away.)

In the light of his changing theology, Luther objected to the principle of what Tetzel was doing. You could, in effect, be buying salvation. As Luther also pointed out in his *Theses*, 'If the Pope had control over the souls in purgatory, why doesn't he open the gate and let them all out?'[42] If he truly had the power, he could do so – and for free!

However, the point was a more important one than a

dig at the financial grasping of the Pope. As George has shown, when Luther made his public protest, he was thereby 'catapulted into a major confrontation with the Roman Church of his day. In the course of that struggle he issued a decisive *no* to the entire papal system.'[43] Luther was not doing so just for the sake of rebellion though, but for that of what he believed to be the 'true ancient church'.

Luther, outraged by Tetzel's activities, wrote to Archbishop Albert of Mainz on 31 October 1517, the date on which Protestant historians traditionally hold that the Reformation began. Luther told Albert that people believed 'the souls leave purgatory as soon as they put the money in the chest'.[44]

The great debate

Luther then prepared 95 theses, or articles for academic discussion. The key thing is that they were intended by him for university debate – he did not mean them to go further, let alone start a major revolution! (Some historians even doubt the story that he pinned them to the door of the church in Wittenberg.)[45]

Let us look at some of the thesis statements before going on to discuss their revolutionary relevance.[46] (Luther's numbering is maintained here.)

1. When our Lord Jesus Christ said 'Repent' ... he meant that the whole life of believers should be one of repentance.

6. The pope can remit no guilt, but only declare and confirm that it has been remitted by God.

27. There is no divine authority for preaching that the soul flies out of purgatory as soon as the money clinks in the collecting box.

81-82. This wanton preaching of pardons makes it difficult for learned men to guard the respect due to the Pope against false accusations or at least from the keen criticisms of the laity. For example why does the Pope not empty purgatory for the sake of holy love? This would be the most righteous of reasons. Meanwhile he redeems innumerable souls for sordid money in order to build St. Peter's, a most trivial reason.

The main import of what Luther was saying here was entirely revolutionary. Theses no. 81-82 can be put in a reforming category. The Pope was misusing his power for financial gain.

But look again at nos. 6 and 17. They go much further than the idea of simple 'reform'. As Hillerbrand has put it, what Luther was actually doing was going well beyond mere reform, because

the real aim of the Protestant Reformation was surely not so much 'reform' as 'reinterpretation' of the Gospels, and it was characterized before long by an inimical stance toward the Catholic church. The Reformation may have built on earlier expressions of reform sentiment; in the final analysis, however, the Reformation introduced an element of discontinuity into these efforts.[47]

For what Luther was doing, little though he realised the full weight of it at the time, was to undermine the very foundations of the Catholic Church and the authority of the Pope himself.

Luther's radical view of the powers of the Pope can be seen in No. 6. In making clear that it is God, not the Pope, who can *effectively* forgive sins, we can see how Luther was, as we saw earlier, completely undermining the entire penitential/mediatory position of medieval Christendom, something that someone as holy and devout as St. Francis of Assisi had not done.

No. 27 tells us: there is 'no divine authority' for what the Pope is saying. Here we see the beginnings of *sola scriptura* – 'by scripture alone'. The entire edifice of the Catholic Church was built on the authority of tradition equalling that of Scripture, and the Pope was at the apex of the authority structure. So now Luther proposes that scripture alone, not the accumulated wisdom and authority of Mother Church, is the real final and absolute authority for the Christian believer. It is also evident implicitly, I think, in the May 1517 Luther letter quoted earlier. Luther writes about Tetzel's claims that there 'is no *divine authority* for preaching that the soul flies out of purgatory as soon as the money clinks in the collecting box'.

Once again, the entire authority structure of medieval Christendom is being undermined because it rested on precisely the claim that the Pope *did* have such an authority, a power which, Luther was now making clear, had no scriptural warrant from God and, therefore, no warrant at all. While Luther may not have realised it fully that October day back in 1517, he was doing something so radical that, as one historian puts it, he 'provoked a schism in Western Christendom which has not yet been healed.'[48]

The key to the theological message of the theses can be seen in what Luther wrote when he said:

When a man believes himself to be utterly lost, light breaks. Peace comes in the word of Christ through faith. He who does not have this is lost even though he be absolved a million times by the pope, and he who does have it may not wish to be released from purgatory, for true contrition seeks penalty. Christians should be encouraged to bear the cross. He who is baptised into Christ must be as a sheep for the slaughter. The merits of Christ are vastly more potent when they bring crosses than when they bring remissions.[49]

Luther did not mention justification by faith *as such* in his *Theses*. It is also vital to remember that he did not intend them to be anything more than a debate among academics like himself. It was others who took up his views, ran with them, and, through the newly discovered means of printing, spread them throughout Europe.

One can argue, though, that justification by faith was strongly *implicit*.[50] Take the first thesis: 'When our Lord Jesus Christ said 'repent' ... he meant that the whole of life should be one of repentance.'

Luther's teaching in these theses spread rapidly, with at least a thousand people reading the three editions of them printed in 1517 alone.[51] They also spread internationally: by March 1518, Erasmus sent the English lawyer Sir Thomas More a copy. The Swiss Reformer Zwingli was distributing them in his country, and in 1519 a Swiss printer in Basel shipped 500 copies to Spain and France. Doctors at the famous Paris University, The Sorbonne, were reading Luther quite openly.

Storming the Papacy

By 1519, Catholic theologians had realised that Luther was challenging the very basis of the Pope's authority. A debate between the Dominican friar, Johann Eck, on the one hand, and Luther and his colleague Carlstadt, on the other, was convened at Leipzig. Here Eck was able to trick Luther into sympathy for the fifteenth-century Bohemian heretic, Jan Hus: a bad move, since the other Saxon prince, Duke George the Bearded, a staunch Catholic, remembered how Hussite troops had on several occasions devastated Saxon territory.

As Luther recalled on 20 July 1519, when Eck likened him to Hus, he defended himself, saying,

> Here I publicly asserted that some articles were condemned at the Council of Constance [in 1415, when Hus was martyred] in a godless manner, since they were taught openly and clearly by Augustine, Paul and even Christ himself.[52]

Once more, Luther is undermining the basis of the Catholic Church, as Eck recognised. Eck himself strongly disliked the abuse of indulgences, and would, Luther wrote, 'have agreed with me in all points had I not debated about the authority of the pope'.[53]

Luther was not, at this early stage, going all out for public controversy. He was amazed at the venom with which he was attacked, for as he wrote to Pope Leo X in 1520:

> It is a mystery to me how my theses ... were spread to so many places.... What shall I do now? I cannot recall my theses and yet their popularity makes me hated. . . . I am no great scholar.... Necessity forces me to be a honking goose among singing swans.[54]

Slowly but surely the robust attacks upon him by his Catholic opponents forced him to think through the dramatic logical conclusions to what he was saying. The result of his ponderings came in three pamphlets which he produced in 1520, and it was in that year that the real theological origins of the Reformation can more truly be said to have begun.

The first of these, written in the internationally scholarly language of Latin, was *On the Babylonian Captivity of the Church*. It was in reading the defence of Papal authority, he wrote, that he understood that the Pope not merely had no divine authority, but no human authority either.

This led on to some other major consequences.

'The first thing for me to do,' he wrote, 'is to deny that there are seven sacraments and for the present to propound three: baptism, penance and the Lord's Supper.'[55] (He was later to drop penance, leaving just two.)

Further, both elements of communion were to be open to the laity – bread and wine – and was called 'communion in both kinds'. This was at the heart of Hussite teaching, and Luther was being very bold in resurrecting it.

But it is also interesting to look at the basis of what he is saying. His teaching on the Mass was firmly based upon his understanding of Scripture.

'It is plain that our salvation begins in our faith.... From all of which you will see that nothing else than faith is needed....There is no scriptural warrant whatever for regarding marriage as a Sacrament.'[56]

Luther now came on to his explosive teaching on ministry: the resurrection of Peter's doctrine in his Epistles of the priesthood of all believers.[57]

Ordination was unknown as a Sacrament to the church of Christ's time.... Now we who have been baptised are all uniformly priests by virtue of that very fact. The only addition received by the priests is the office of preaching, and even this with our consent.... Those whom we call priests are really ministers of the Word and chosen by us; they fulfil their entire office in our name. The priesthood is simply the ministry of the Word.... The function of the priest is to preach; if he does not preach he is no more a priest than the picture of a man is a man.[58]

His most explosive tract, however, was not written in scholarly Latin but in German, and was thus capable of being read by everyone (although not therefore by scholars in other countries, for whom it would have to be translated).[59] This was *On the Liberty of the Christian Man*. This mentioned both justification by faith, *sola fidei*, and also how Christians should behave. It was also widely misunderstood, particularly by peasants and townspeople who misunderstood its primarily *spiritual* message, and interpreted it in a politically radical light.

He wrote:

I shall set down the following two propositions concerning the freedom and the bondage of the Spirit: A Christian is a perfectly free lord of all, subject to none. A Christian is a perfectly dutiful servant of all, subject to all.... One thing and only one thing is necessary for Christian life, righteousness and freedom. That one thing is the most holy Word of God, the Gospel of Christ....The Word of God cannot be received and cherished by any works whatever, but only by faith. Therefore it is clear that, as the soul needs only the Word of God for its life and righteousness, so it is justified by faith alone and not by any works. Thus, the believing soul by means of the pledge of its faith is free in Christ, free from all sins, secure against death and hell, and is endowed with eternal righteousness.... Yes, since faith alone suffices for salvation, I need nothing except faith exercising the power and domination of its own liberty. This is the inestimable power and liberty of Christians.[60]

We are free by faith alone! The Church, the whole edifice of medieval Catholicism and the very power upon which it rested, was now cut out completely.

As Euan Cameron has so eloquently expressed it, Luther was engaged not simply in an attack on abuses within the Church, as the internal reform movements were trying to do, but something entirely new: a fundamental undermining of the Church's core operation, that of being the intermediary mediator of the means of God's grace to ordinary people.[61]

Cameron writes that,

> the remorselessly coherent logic of the basic protestant message about human salvation entailed and demanded that one abandoned the search for quantitative 'grace' through acts of ritual, ceremonial piety done in the face of Mother Church. If souls were not saved by acquiring through religious exercises the 'grace' to atone for one's sins, then the entire mechanism which channelled, measured out and dispensed such 'grace' was redundant.[62]

It is not surprising that when Erasmus read the *Babylonian Captivity* pamphlet, he commented that the 'breach is irreparable'.[63]

In relation to the debate with which we began this chapter, it is the full logical consequence of both *sola fide* and *sola scriptura* that makes Luther entirely new, a revolutionary and not just a reformer. In the Papal Bull, *Exsurge Domine* of 15th June 1520, with which the Pope condemned Luther and his teaching, it is not surprising that the Papal metaphor about Luther was of a 'wild boar' in the 'vineyard'![64]

For as Cameron puts it, the older reformers had never

questioned 'fundamentally the received economy of salvation' in the way that Luther was now doing.[65]

He writes,

> Where the old priests had retreated into their privileges and cloisters, the reformers went into the squares and council chambers and asked for lay support. Instead of burying a dogma in a technical jargon, they translated it and insisted that any layman learn its tenets.[66]

As Luther wrote in *On the Liberty of the Christian Man*,

> Not only are we the freest of kings, we are also priests forever ... for as priests we are worthy to appear before God to pray for others and to teach one another divine things.... You will ask, 'If all who are in the church are priests, how do those whom we now call priests differ from laypeople?'[67]

Luther's response was that such men are merely those

> who should according to the ministry of the Word serve others and teach them the faith of Christ and the freedom of believers. Although we are all equally priests, we cannot all publicly minister and teach.[68]

This, naturally, ended the entire 'penitential cycle' on which the medieval church's power was based.[69] This is what was new.

So how was it that someone as radical as this was not burned at the stake, as Hus had been? It is here that we must come on to the vital *political* development of the *spiritual* revolution.[70]

Luther and the German nation

Hus died at the stake; Luther lived and died peacefully. Why the difference?

The answer, humanly speaking, is *political*. Luther was protected in a way in which previous Reformers had failed to be. When it became clear that the Papacy was unhappy with Luther, he was protected by his political overlord, Elector Frederick the Wise. Spiritually speaking, it is difficult to know exactly where Frederick stood. His fame rooted, for example, on his gigantic collection of 'holy relics', most of which would probably not pass scrutiny today as genuine. But Frederick seems to have been keen to protect one of his own, both from the Pope and from Frederick's political overlord, the Holy Roman Emperor.

Here, Electoral politics helped. When the Emperor, Maximilian, died in 1519, the Papacy was nervous at the prospect of his grandson, Charles of Burgundy, succeeding him: Charles ruled not only over the present-day Netherlands, but also over Spain, present-day Austria and large parts of present-day Italy. The Popes were the secular rulers of much of Central Italy (the Papal States) and, as political rulers, were naturally nervous at Charles assuming the throne of the Holy Roman Empire (of present-day Germany, in effect) as well. Frederick the Wise, being an Elector, had power to influence the election, so the Pope had, temporarily, to pull his punches.

In the end, Charles became Emperor, as Charles V, and, ironically, was one of the staunchest defenders, in spiritual terms, of Catholicism against Luther. (As we will see in the chapter on Cranmer, Charles was unwittingly to help bring about the Reformation in England, too, since he was the nephew of Henry VIII's first wife, Catherine of Aragon.)

Frederick, like the other Electors, voted for Charles, who had given the largest bribes. But although he owed Charles political allegiance, he was equally loyal to his own, Saxon, *German* subjects. Like many others at the time, Frederick felt the strong appeal of early German nationalism.[71]

Some of Luther's earliest supporters were aggressively nationalist, and prepared, if needs be, to use force. To them, Luther was the champion of German liberty against alien, foreign interference from the Pope many miles away in Rome. Historians and sociologists have argued whether some of these people, such as the knights Ulrich von Hutten and Franz von Sickingen, did so because as a social class, Imperial Knights, owners of only a small domain but with direct allegiance to the Emperor (as opposed to a local Prince or Elector), were in social and economic decline.[72] They were both helpful to Luther, in that they gave him military support, but also unhelpful in that their power base was rather limited. Either way, though, the nationalist feelings which they had for Luther were indicative of a wider mood which, in political terms, was certainly useful in creating a favourable climate for the break with Rome.

Luther rejected an offer of military aid from von Hutten, writing in January 1521:

I am not willing to fight for the gospel with bloodshed. In this sense I have written to [von Hutten]. The world is conquered by the Word, and by the Word the Church is served and rebuilt.[73]

Political help of some kind would be needed, though, and this is why Luther wrote his book in 1520, the *Address to the Christian Nobility of the German Nation*. If, Luther argued, the Church refused to reform itself, it was for the nobility, the political leadership of the Holy Roman Empire, to get the Church to call a council that would implement reform. It was this appeal to the laity that was, as Cameron correctly points out, one of the most critical points of the Reformation:[74] lay power over the Church, undoing centuries of Papal claims to be superior to the laity.[75]

The Diet of Worms

In Luther's dedication in his *Address* he wrote that 'the time for silence is over and the time for speech has come'.[76] Luther was unafraid to speak out, something made more perilous by the formal decree of Papal excommunication against him in January 1521, *Decet Romanum Pontificem*. However, the decree had to be implemented, and here Frederick the Wise was able to bargain on Luther's behalf. The Imperial Diet, the parliament of all the lay and ecclesiastical princes of the Holy Roman Emperor, was meeting that year in Worms. There were strong undercurrents of nationalist sentiment against what some of the Princes felt was Roman corruption, so many of them wanted to hear Luther address them himself. Frederick was able to get Luther a safe conduct, which looked reassuring until one remembers that Hus had had a similar safe conduct to the Council of Constance in 1415, but had ended up being burned at the stake all the same. Luther was clearly in possible danger of his life, but decided to go regardless, saying, 'We will come to Worms in spite of all the gates of hell.'[77]

On 21 April 1521, Luther found himself before the Emperor and assembled Princes. After some debate, Luther was given a chance to recant. The assembly met again the next day. Luther addressed them with words which have gone on to be famous, and which show the bravery of a single man in the face of the combined forces of both Church and State.

Luther declared:[78]

> Since then your Majesty and your lordships desire a simple reply, I will answer without horns and without teeth. Unless I am convicted by Scripture and plain reason – I do not accept the authority of popes and councils, for they have contradicted each other – my conscience is captive to the Word of God. I cannot and I will not recant anything, for to go against conscience is neither right nor safe. God help me! Amen.[79]

Luther repeated his firm stand in private, and left Worms on April 26. Aleander, the Papal representative in Worms, noticed that popular support for Luther was immensely strong. Numerous pamphlets and woodcuts (making use of new printing technology) portrayed Luther in the most glowing terms, almost comparing him to Christ himself.

Despite Luther's eloquence, Charles V was not convinced. He announced himself to be a faithful Catholic, and declared Luther a 'notorious heretic'.[80] Four out of the seven Electors agreed to brand Luther heretical, with two, Frederick the Wise of Saxony, and Ludwig, the Elector Palatine of the Rhine, dissenting.

Although Charles had granted Luther a safe conduct back to Wittenberg, Frederick took no chances. He had Luther kidnapped, and put in a safe castle in his own territories, the Wartburg (the 'safe stronghold' of Luther's famous hymn?). Here Luther was known as 'George' and he even grew a beard to disguise his identity. Frederick might protect him, but others would not. On 8th May, Charles put Luther under ban of the Empire. He was now an outlaw.

If, however, Charles thought that banning Luther would stop the impetus, he was sadly mistaken. As Hillerbrand puts it, Charles, Aleander and the others had 'all failed to sense the profundity of the hour'.[81]

Luther in the Wartburg

Luther was stuck in the Wartburg until March 1522. But he was far from idle, perhaps because constant activity seems to have been in his nature and perhaps too because he was having to cope with terrible bouts of recurrent depression (the exact nature of which we can only speculate about at this distance).

He published editions of his sermons on the Gospels and the Epistles, and a volume on the Magnificat. He continued to write strenuously argued pamphlets in defence of his doctrine of justification by faith.

Above all, though, he began on his great translation of the Bible, with the New Testament appearing six months after his release, in September 1522. (The Old Testament came out later, in 1534.)

Luther's prose has been described as 'a literary event of the first magnitude, for it is the first work of art in German prose'.[82] Luther completed the New Testament in just two and a half months! He reissued it several times, with the 1545 version coming to be regarded as definitive.

The impact of having the Bible *in your own language* cannot be overestimated. It opened up the Bible to a massively greater audience than had hitherto existed. Intelligent, well-educated lay people had long been able to read the Bible for themselves, but only if they knew Latin (the language of the officially approved version), and it was usually only the higher clergy who could read it in the original Greek or Hebrew.

What Luther's translation did was to make it accessible on a large scale to the educated middle classes, who could read their own language but not those languages of the past such as Latin or Greek. As we have seen, the opening of the debate on the nature of the church to the ordinary laity is one of the keys to the whole success of the Reformation. Critical in this, along with Luther's doctrine of the priesthood of all believers, was the ability of leading lay men and women to be able to read the Bible for themselves in their own language.[83]

This was to have much wider repercussions than Luther himself realised at the time. His Bible became a linguistic classic, right down to our own times: Luther's Bible had the same effect on the German language as the Authorised/King James Version in English. Some have also said that the liberating effect of having God's word in their own language created a strong sense of *national* identity, because it was read, in the same version, by people from Schleswig in the north through to Bavaria in the South. Whether or not Luther's German language Bible created a form of proto-nationalism is more contentious.

As Benedict Anderson has written, 'Before the age of print, Rome easily won every war against heresy in Western Europe because it always had better internal lines of communication than its challengers.'[84]

Luther's *Theses*, thanks to printing, spread all over Europe. As Anderson continues,

In the two decades 1520-1540 three times as many books were published *in German* (italics added) as in the period 1500-1520, an astonishing transformation to which Luther was absolutely central. His works represented no less than one third of *all* German language books sold between 1518 and 1525.[85]

Between the New Testament coming out in 1522 and Luther's death in 1546, a total of 430 editions (whole or partial) of his Bible translation appeared.

As two French authors have written, 'We have here for the first time a truly mass readership and a popular literature within *everybody's reach* (italics added).'[86]

As Anderson goes on to show,

In effect, Luther became the first best-selling author so known. Or, to put it another way, the first writer who could 'sell' his new books on the basis of his name. Where Luther led, others quickly followed, opening the colossal religious propaganda war that raged across Europe for the next century.[87]

Critically, as Anderson shows,

In this titanic battle for men's minds, Protestantism was always fundamentally on the offensive, precisely because it knew how to make use of the expanding vernacular print-market being created.[88]

What secular writers like Anderson often omit (as it is not central to the principal political, economic or sociological argument that they are making – in Anderson's case about the rise of modern nationalistic movements) is that the word in *your own language* was central to Luther's *theology* and to his understanding of *sola scriptura*. As he wrote, just around the time of his release from the Wartburg,

> I opposed Indulgences and all the papists, but never with force. I simply taught, preached, and wrote God's word; otherwise I did nothing. And while I slept or drank Wittenberg beer with my friends..., the Word so greatly weakened the Papacy that no prince or emperor ever inflicted such losses on it. I did nothing; the Word did everything....[89]

This is not just modesty on Luther's part – *sola scriptura* was at the heart of the whole thing. It was the article of faith upon which Luther was able to denounce the entire penitential edifice of medieval Catholicism. Everything rested on what he called 'the sure rule of God's word', for if, as he said,

> anyone of the saintly fathers can show that his interpretation is based on Scripture, and if Scripture proves that this is the way it should be interpreted, then that interpretation is right. If this is not the case, I must not believe him.[90]

Scripture is not merely pivotal to understanding what Luther, and indeed the whole Reformation as espoused by the other four subjects of this book, is all about; it is also essential to understanding the effect on ordinary Christians. Luther, through getting the Bible translated, did not intend it to come out unexplained. Preaching, expounding the word of God, became an integral part of Protestantism, the sermon part of the core of Sunday worship.[91]

Furthermore, the Bible had an essential message at its heart, and this was the good news of Jesus Christ. Luther wrote:

He who would read the Bible must simply take heed that he does not err, for the Scripture may permit itself to be stretched and led, but let no one lead it according to his own inclinations but let him lead it to the source, that is, the cross of Christ. Then he will surely strike the centre.[92]

In one fell swoop, Luther despatched all the fanciful, multi-layered, complex and allegorical interpretations of the Bible which so littered the Middle Ages. The simplest, most straightforward, interpretation was the best.

The preaching in your own language of the Bible in your own language had one other major effect on the laity which, as Cameron has so correctly pointed out, made the Reformation both more acceptable and successful.[93] Within three years of Luther's appearance at Worms, and despite his own temporary incarceration in the Wartburg, preachers were enthusiastically spreading Luther's teaching all over Germany, and proving quite unstoppable in the process. Why was this? Just as important – how was popular Lutheranism not politically crushed after 1522? For numerous cities, whose rulers were often elected wealthy merchants who owed direct allegiance to the Emperor, were allowing Luther's doctrines to spread freely, as were bold Princes such as Frederick the Wise.

Cameron has, I think, come up with the answer. He writes that from

being hesitant trespassers on the margins of the spiritual domain, laymen were actually invited to judge issues at the very heart of their dealings with the Almighty, and by clerics at that! When one views the choice open to laymen – rulers or people – in the early days of the Reformation's spread, it is not the fact that people adopted the movement which is puzzling; it is that there were anywhere in Europe people loyal enough to the old catholicism to nip the new movement in the bud before it was too late.[94]

Lay empowerment was, I feel, at the heart of the success of the Reformation. To Luther, this was a *spiritual* issue, as it was to many ordinary people and to the genuinely disinterested among the secular rulers. But Luther had also empowered the Princes, seeing rulers as 'the left hand of God'[95] (the Church itself being the right hand). For those

> who exercise secular authority have been baptized like the rest of us, and have the same faith and the same gospel; therefore we must admit that they are priests and bishops. They discharge their office as an office of the Christian community, and for the benefit of that community.[96]

German rulers, with memories of Emperor Henry VI having to grovel before the Pope at Canossa back in the Middle Ages, would have found such words heady and liberating: the Church was not superior to a secular prince, or city council!

Space does not permit a detailed examination of exactly which city or principality went over to the Reformation, or did not, and why.[97]

What we need to do here is to establish a *principle*, which is that lay empowerment not only helped to spread the Reformation, but also, I would argue, prevented it from being wiped out. Whatever Charles V's opposition to the Reformation might have been – and he never gave up his hostility to it – the fact is that Luther, unlike Hus, died peacefully in his bed. Enough city councillors and lay princes supported Luther to enable the nascent Protestant faith (as it soon became known, because of princely *protests* against Charles' wishes) to survive. Those of us who are Protestant Christians today might well see the hand of God in all this, but for those wanting secular reasons for Lutheran survival, I think that this is as convincing an argument as any.

The fact that more Princes and city councillors did not turn to Luther can be attributed to the onset of the Peasants Revolts, which erupted in 1524, and which were especially vicious in Thuringia, the district of Germany in which Luther lived.

Luther had, when speaking *spiritually*, made clear that the Christian was a 'perfectly free lord of all, subject to none'.[98] The problem was that many peasants interpreted this *politically* as well – that they were no longer subject to their political overlords – in a way which Luther had not intended. In addition, one of Martin Luther's leading followers, Thomas Muntzer, also added a strong politically radical side to the spiritual message of liberation. Muntzer threatened violent revolution, and Luther saw before himself the fate of the followers of Hus in Bohemia, where the desire for spiritual reform swiftly led to military action and widespread bloodshed. Luther thereupon denounced Muntzer, who in turn violently denounced Luther.

Luther's initial response to peasant grievances was a friendly one – in April 1525 he wrote his *Friendly Admonition to Peace Concerning the Twelve Articles of the Peasants* (their manifesto). Many of the demands were reasonable and were based on rights that peasants had lost over time to some of the more rapacious incursions of their political or economic overlords.

However, Luther discovered that the peasants were using

the Gospels in their demands and in their revolt against their secular rulers. Luther had written in 1523, in his book, *On Earthly Government*, that we should obey the secular authorities, since they are placed there by God himself. So, with the peasants now using the Bible *against* such authorities, Luther wrote that even if the grievances were 'proper and right according to the natural law, you have forgotten the Christian law, since you do not seek to obtain them with patience and prayer to God, as becomes Christian men, but with impatience and blasphemy to force the authorities'.[99] Three weeks after this Luther denounced the peasant rebels in the most forceful of language, in his tract *Against the Murderous and Thieving Hordes of Peasants*.

In fact, the peasants were routed on 15 May 1525 at the battle of Frankenhausen, and their rebellion was repressed with the utmost savagery and brutality by the authorities.

Luther's tract was, therefore, unfortunately timed, since it alienated him from many of the peasants who might otherwise have supported him.[100] Large numbers of peasants, though, stayed loyal to the Reformation, joining the growing number of radicals who are known to us as Anabaptists. While space (and the choice of the particular five Reformers) in this book does not permit a detailed examination of Anabaptist history, it is true to say that Anabaptists had a more radical, separatist view of Church and State, as well as their doctrine of limiting church membership to believers only. With neither of these views was Luther happy,[101] and when some Anabaptists, such as those in Münster in 1534-1535, erupted into violent rebellion and wild behaviour, the breach was complete.

Luther was also blamed for peasant excesses by some of the more cautious princes. Catholic rulers tended to get together out of common concern for things getting out of hand. Protestant princes, seeing Catholic rulers getting together, decided that they ought to do likewise, for self-protection – it was still politically risky at this stage to follow Luther too openly. Events, everyone realised might come to a head at the next Imperial Diet, in Speyer in 1526. As Hillerbrand comments:

> Therefore, the two parties of the religious controversy began to face one another, not merely as proponents of differing theological points of view, but also as warriors preparing for battle. The Reformation became a political phenomenon and the character of the course of events changed. If the first phase had been the popular response to Luther's proclamation, and if the second phase had been characterized by the haphazard administration of the Edict of Worms [against Luther] in individual territories, the third phase brought the emergence of two political blocs, the one loyal to the Catholic church, the other committed to the new faith.[102]

While these great political events were taking place, something just as important was happening in the life of Luther. He got married!

The Reformation saw major change especially in Protestant countries of that great medieval institution, monasticism, a celibate way of life which involved renouncing the possibility of marriage.[103] The traditional teaching was that marriage was somehow second rate. Not only that, but the whole idea that there was a theologically and spiritually superior class of being – celibate monks and nuns – vanished with the influx of the doctrine of the priesthood of all believers. You did not have to be a monk or nun to be truly godly – *all* believers could now attain the goal, even those who did the humblest and most menial of tasks.

Such doctrines dramatically heightened the role of women, no longer seen as inferior. Countless nuns found themselves released from monastic seclusion and one of them was a woman of exceptionally strong character, Katherine von Bora.

A group of nuns had forsaken their vows, and re-entered normal life. All but one had been found husbands – that one was Katherine. In 1525 Luther, now aged 42, married her, much to the amazement of all his friends.

Katherine was no pushover, and proved to be a strong lady very much in her own right. The Luthers had six children and the happiness of their domestic life became well-known. Soon the former monk amazed himself by becoming an example of wedded bliss, though he soon found that being married to a wife with a mind of her own was not easy! As he put it, marriage was a 'school for character'.[104] It was just as well though: Luther had no concept of money and was over-inclined to generosity. Katherine put the household firmly in order and was able to generate some reliable income. She became not just a superb manager, but also an expert brewer, a semi-qualified doctor (extraordinary for those times) and an authoritative farmer, running the newly acquired family farm at Zulsdorf.

Luther and his family were constantly inundated with visitors wanting to see the great man. His 'table talk' became famous and was later published. His earthy peasant origins came out in the slightly coarse way[105] in which he spoke: 'The only portion of the human anatomy which the Pope has had to leave uncontrolled is his rear end.'[106]

Sometimes, though, the jokes were at his own expense:

'They are trying to make me into a fixed star. I am an irregular planet.'[107]

However, life then was much rougher and far more basic than it is now. Public hygiene was much less widespread, with many an open gutter in the street. One day, when Luther had been unable to attend a service, his wife mentioned that 'the church was so full it stank'. 'Yes,' replied Luther, 'they had manure on their boots,' which they almost certainly had![108]

The year that Luther married, his political protector Frederick the Wise died. Fortunately for Luther, his successors as Electors of Saxony proved to be strong supporters, as did Philip the Magnanimous, ruler of Hesse (and ancestor of the Mountbatten family, thus also of Queen Elizabeth II's husband, another Philip) and Albert of Brandenburg, a relative of the Archbishop of Mainz, whose need for money had set things in motion back in 1517. These, and other princes, along with about twenty cities were to give solid political support to Luther throughout the difficult times ahead.

Charles V remained hostile to Luther, but now found that he could not crush the new movement as easily as he might have liked. So when the Diet met again in Speyer in 1526, Luther had his allies.[109]

This meant that the Edict of Worms was suspended pending the meeting of a national council. Each Prince was to decide how to act within his own territory, as before God and his Emperor. In other words, it was a stalemate.

Furthermore, Charles was away from Speyer itself. He had wars to conduct against the French in Italy (which included an Imperial seizure of Rome), Spain to rule over as King, and the Turks to keep out, both out of the

Mediterranean in his capacity as a ruler of much of Italy, and out of Central Europe in his role as ruler of Austria (along with his brother Ferdinand, who was nominal King of Hungary). Nowadays we would call this 'overstretch',[110] with Charles having to fight too many enemies on too many fronts, all at the same time, with nowhere near enough resources to do so.

Charles had to stay away for a while longer, and, as a result, a temporary truce ended up becoming more permanent, allowing Lutheranism to consolidate both spiritually and politically in its strongholds – although not to expand, since Catholic Princes continued to enforce the Edict of Worms rigorously in their own domains. In fact, if you look at a map of Germany today, the areas that are currently Protestant and currently Catholic are not entirely unlike those areas which were predominantly Lutheran or Catholic back in the 1520s. Brandenburg remains essentially Protestant, Bavaria mainly Catholic. The Reformation was becoming increasingly politicised.

Much of this was due to Charles' absences on account of his other wars.[111]

[N]othing happened, and the truce became a peace. The religious schism developed to a state beyond repair. Here lies the tragedy of Charles V. His absence from Germany, prompted by his complex involvement in Spanish and, indeed, all of European politics, created a vacuum in Germany and decisively influenced the fate of the Reformation. Charles, if anyone, should have been the one to stem the tide of the Lutheran heresy. But he was far away ... waging war against his archfoe Francis I [King of France].... In short, his concerns were those of the *rey catholico* of Spain rather than of the *Kaiser* of Germany.[112]

(As we shall see in the Cranmer chapter, Charles' Italian wars against the French were also to have a major impact, albeit unintended, on the English reformation, by hampering the Pope at a critical moment in Henry's desire for a divorce from Charles' aunt Catherine). Luther was able to consolidate the Reformation in Saxony and in other territories that had turned to the new Protestant faith.

Luther produced two catechisms, or summaries of essential Christian knowledge, in 1529: the large one for adults and the small one for children. The large one was overtly polemic, clearly 'Protestant' in doctrine – a word we can now use properly since it was first used in that year to describe those German Princes who 'protested' against the Emperor's strongly Catholic line at the second Diet to be held at Speyer.

Luther especially intended the catechisms to be used at home, for parents to instruct their children (and the family servants) in the rudiments of the faith.

As he wrote,

Do not think the catechism is a little thing to be read hastily and cast aside. Although I am a doctor [of theology], I have to do just as a child and say word for word for every morning.... To be occupied with God's Word helps against the world, the flesh and the Devil, and all bad thoughts.[113]

Luther was involved in many other theological discussions at the time, notably on the vexed issue of what precisely happened at the Communion Table, or Eucharist. Protestants united only in rejecting the Catholic view that Christ was literally in the elements themselves (transubstantiation). Luther believed strongly, though, that Christ was nevertheless present at Communion, whereas the leading Swiss Reformer, Zwingli, argued for a more symbolic view. Each party claimed scriptural support.

In a book as short as this, it is not possible to go into too much detail, so I will deal with the issue in the chapter on Zwingli (also in order to avoid repetition).[114] The main thing to say here is that the strong disagreement over Communion shows that already the new Protestant version of Christian faith was evidencing the splits that have since become its hallmark: splits over issues other than the basic life and work of Jesus Christ. We now take the vast multiplicity of Protestant denominations for granted: for the early Reformers such splits were both new and somewhat disturbing.

The minds of the Protestants were also concentrated because Charles V was now, at last, after many wars, defeats and victories, able to return to Germany. A great meeting was to be convened at Augsburg, in 1530.

Luther was still, so far as Charles was concerned, an outlaw, so was forbidden to come. This meant that the gathering of Lutherans, to put forward a united, considered document before the Diet, had to meet without Luther being present. Instead the task was left in the charge of his close friend, but much more irenic and less confrontational follower, Philip Melanchthon.[115] Luther meanwhile had to wait in the safety of the Elector of Saxony's castle of Coburg (the British Royal family and many other present-day royal houses descend from Luther's key political supporters of this time).

Melanchthon was keen to find a way in which the two sides could be reconciled, and heal the breach within Germany between Protestant and Catholic. The Augsburg Confession, as it is known, is therefore a peace-making document. Despite this wish for accord though, certain items were non-negotiable from the Protestant side: while the Pope's authority was not explicitly denied, 'on the doctrinal side justification by faith alone was asserted and transubstantiation denied'.[116]

As Luther's biographer Roland Bainton has put it, although the Anabaptists and Zwinglians did not go along with all the Augsburg Confession's views, the Confession

> did much to consolidate Protestantism and set it over against Catholicism. One might take the date June 25, 1530, the day when the Augsburg Confession was publicly read, as the death day of the Holy Roman Empire. From this day forward the two confessions stood over against each other, poised for conflict.[117]

Already the Protestants, led by Philip of Hesse, had made defensive alliances.[118] Charles gave the Protestants a year to submit. On 27 February 1531, the Protestants founded the league of Schmalkalden, ready to defend their faith by military means if necessary. Now the Reformation was becoming even more political than before. Charles, however, had to wait another fifteen years before he could be in any remote position to launch a military counter-attack. The ever-present danger of Muslim invasion prevented him from taking the aggressive steps that he might have preferred. By that time Luther himself was dead and Protestantism far too firmly entrenched. Charles was able to prevent further territory from being lost, but he was never able fully to reclaim for Catholicism the lands which Luther had won for the Protestant cause.

One biographer of Luther has written that 'the last sixteen years of Luther's life, from the Augsburg

Confession in 1530 to his death in 1546, are commonly treated more cursorily by biographers than the early period'.[119] They are certainly less heroic years, because Luther was now far more of a consolidator, building up a new kind of church, than a pioneer, doing something revolutionary and wholly new. He remained, too, under the ban of the Empire (Charles never relented), and this meant that his personal scope for travel was drastically restricted – others, such as Melanchthon, would have to do the wider journeys. This is not to say that Luther was inactive – far from it. He wrote as much as ever. Sadly he continued to vilify the most radical Protestants – the Anabaptists – and he wrote pamphlets that would now certainly be regarded as rabidly anti-Semitic.[120] In doing so he was, of course, reflecting the virulent intolerance of his day, something with which we in the twenty-first century are, hopefully, very uncomfortable, but, after the atrocities of the Holocaust and Kosovo, all too familiar. After 1537, he was also rather ill, and often in terrible pain.

He died on 18 February 1546, in the town of Eisleben, where he had been born. He died peacefully, not martyred. His Church had survived – all those of us who are Protestants today are his legacy. He was that rare creature – a successful revolutionary.

As J. I. Packer has written:

Careful Calvin orchestrated Protestant theology most skilfully, but fertile Martin Luther wrote most of the tunes.... Luther learned from the apostles Paul and John that our holy Creator saves sinners by imparting through his Word a transforming knowledge of Jesus Christ. Believers know Christ as the divine Lover who died for their sins, who rose again to conquer 'principalities and powers', and now as mediator secures to them the gift of righteousness – pardon of guilt, acceptance as God's children, and sure hope of reward. From this faith – knowledge of Christ and his benefits flows the whole of Christian living: repentance, communion with God, and good works, all in conscious freedom from the soul-destroying necessity of earning God's continued favour by self-effort. Such was Luther's gospel of justification by faith only.[121]

References

1. FFA/DW, p. 6.
   2. Ibid., p. ix.
   3. Ibid., p. x.
   4. Ibid., p. x.
   5. Ibid., pp. x-xi.
   6. Ibid., p. 3.
   7. Ibid., p. 7.
   8. Ibid., p. 20.
   9. Cameron, p. 19.
   10. Ibid., p. 15.
   11. Ibid., pp. 20-48.
   12. For details of this important movement, see Philip McNair, 'Seeds of Renewal' in *The Lion/Eerdmans Handbook to the History of Christianity* (London and Grand Rapids, 1977) pp. 346-359, esp.355-34.
   13. See Hans J. Hillerbrand, *The World of the Reformation* (London, 1973) p. 12, commenting on the work of E. Erikson, *Young Man Luther* (New York, 1957).
   14. E. G. Rupp, 'Martin Luther' in *Encyclopaedia Britannica*, Macropaedia, vol. 11, 15th edn. (Chicago, 1975) p. 188.
   15. Philip McNair, 'Seeds of Renewal', pp. 353-357.
   16. Roland H. Bainton, *Here I Stand* (Nashville and London, 1955) p. 15. In order to avoid too many endnotes, I will not cite sources for all the *narrative* parts of Luther's life. When it comes to debates, interpretations and disagreements, I will give the fullest references possible.
   17. Gerhard Ebeling, *Luther: An Introduction to His Thought*

(London: Fontana edition, 1972) pp. 33-34.

 18. Rupp, 'Martin Luther', p. 188.

 19. Bainton, *Here I Stand,* p. 27.

 20. Timothy George, *The Theology of the Reformers* (Nashville, 1988) pp. 64-68.

 21. Ibid., p. 65.

 22. Ibid.

 23. Ibid. Luther was grateful to him, saying subsequently, 'If Staupitz had not helped me out, I would have been swallowed up and left in hell' (p. 63).

 24. For more detailed study on this, see George's book and Euan Cameron's *History of the European Reformation* (Oxford, 1991); above all read Alister McGrath's magisterial *Intellectual Origins of the European Reformation* (Oxford, 1987), and on Luther specifically, his *Luther's Theology of the Cross* (Oxford, 1985).

 25. R. Stupperich in 'Martin Luther' in *Eerdmans Handbook*, pp. 362-363 says that only Christ has had more written about him than Luther.

 26. For example, Cameron, pp. 38-49, who shows the strength of those wanting reform from within.

 27. FFA/DW, pp. 82-87 discusses this in some detail.

 28. See, for example, Owen Chadwick, *The Reformation* (London, 1964) p. 45.

 29. Those wanting to examine this in detail can look at Cameron, pp. 168-174, who understands the difficult task of trying to put chronology together. Regardless of *when* it happened, though, *what* happened was revolutionary.

 30. Bainton, *Here I Stand*, pp. 49-50; see also Ebeling, pp. 39-41; James Atkinson, 'Reform' in *The Lion/ Eerdmans Handbook to the History of Christianity*, p. 366. I am using Bainton's translation. The one in Ebeling is slightly fuller and translates German words differently: i.e., *righteous* instead of *just*. Why not look at several translations and compare them? See also George, p. 62.

 31. FFA/DW, p. 85.

 32. George, p. 72.

 33. Cameron, p. 121.

 34. See, e.g., Rupp, p. 189.

 35. Cameron, p. 111.

36. Chadwick, p. 46.

37. For example, George, p. 86.

38. Such as Ebeling, pp. 59-60 and Chadwick, pp. 11-24.

39. See George, p. 88. The *other reformers* here refers to those trying to reform the Church from the inside, which, as George points out, was arguably Luther's own position until around 1520, when the full logic of his position, and the angry Papal reaction to him, made such a stance *from within* untenable. See also Chadwick, p. 39.

40. Hillerbrand, pp. 14-16. Wittenberg was in the Archdiocese of Magdeburg and thus under Albert's ecclesiastical control.

41. Chadwick, p. 42.

42. George, p. 88.

43. Ibid., p. 86.

44. Pamela Johnson and Bob Scribner, *The Reformation in Germany and Switzerland* (Cambridge and New York, 1993) p. 12.

45. Ibid., p. 13.

46. Ibid., pp. 13-14. Bainton, *Here I Stand*, pp. 60-64. Cameron, pp. 100-110.

47. Hillerbrand, p. 148.

48. George, p. 86.

49. Bainton, *Here I Stand*, p. 63.

50. Catherwood, *Crash Course*, p. 99. Very few books on the Reformation give precise details of the theses themselves, but instead give accounts of the reaction to them or the theology behind them. However, the full text of the *Theses* and Luther's other works are available in the following English edition: Jaroslav Pelikan and Helmut T. Lehmann, *Works of Martin Luther*, vols. 1-54, St. Louis and Philadelphia, 1955-1968.

51. Johnson and Scribner, p. 13; Hillerbrand, p. 149.

52. Johnson and Scribner, p. 16. Bainton, *Here I Stand*, pp. 85-92.

53. Johnson and Scribner, p. 16.

54. Ibid., p. 17.

55. Ibid., p. 17. Bainton, *Here I Stand*, pp. 105-110.

56. Johnson and Scribner, p. 18.

57. I Peter 2:9. It always strikes me as ironic that it was *Peter*, whose successor the Popes claimed to be, who should be the person who taught in Scripture the doctrine which Luther resurrected, of the priesthood of all believers!

58. Johnson and Scribner, p. 18.

59. Hillerbrand, p. 149.

60. Johnson and Scribner, p. 19

61. Cameron, p. 418.

62. Ibid.

63. Bainton, *Here I Stand*, p. 105.

64. Ibid. p. 114.

65. Cameron, p. 420. See pp. 419-421 for the fuller context.

66. Ibid., p. 420

67. Johnston and Scribner, p. 19.

68. Ibid.

69. Cameron, pp. 79-80.

70. For a good discussion of this, see Hillerbrand, pp. ix-x and 1-10.

71. When exactly nationalism began is a point hotly disputed by historians and sociologists, with no real effective consensus emerging. For a more detailed look at this, see my book *Why the Nations Rage*, where I attempt to distil the essence of the debate.

72. Bainton, *Here I Stand*, p. 104. See pp. 100-104 and Cameron, pp. 200-202 for more details of this debate.

73. Bainton, *Here I Stand*, p. 104.

74. Cameron, p. 422.

75. *Crash Course*, p. 72; Hans Rosenberg on 'Pope Innocent III' in *Eerdmans/Lion Handbook*, p. 255, for a look at the political claims of Popes Gregory VII and Innocent III.

76. Ebeling, p. 62.

77. Hillerbrand, p. 23.

78. *Here I Stand*, p. 144. See also Cameron, p. 103.

79. Rupp, p. 192 says that the famous words, 'here I stand' are possibly mythical but well encapsulate Luther's authentic response to pressure. Bainton thinks that the words may be genuine.

80. Bainton, *Here I Stand*, p. 145.

81. Hillerbrand, p. 26.

82. T. Lane, 'A Flood of Bibles' in the *Eerdmans/Lion Handbook*, p. 368, quoting an unnamed source.

83. Ebeling, pp. 180-181; Roland Bainton, *The Reformation of the Sixteenth Century*, 2nd rev. edn. (Boston, 1985), pp. 44-47; Cameron, pp. 103 and 106-107; George, pp. 83-85.

84. See, for example, Benedict Anderson, *Imagined Communities*, 2nd rev. edn. (London and New York, 1991), p. 39 (also p. 40).

85. Ibid., p. 39.

86. Lucien Febure and Henri-Jean Martin, *The Coming of the Book* (London, 1976, English translation; French original, *L'Apparition du Livre*, Paris, 1958) quoted in Anderson, pp. 39 and p. 208). But see Cameron, p. 6, for a useful perspective: print *helped* the Reformation, but did not *cause* it.

87. Anderson, pp. 39-40.

88. Ibid.

89. Cameron, pp. 106-107.

90. George, p. 82.

91. Ibid., pp. 79-86.

92. Ibid., p. 83.

93. Cameron, pp. 107-108.

94. Ibid., p. 312. See also pp. 310-313, especially p. 311.

95. George, pp. 100-101; see also Ebeling, pp. 175-191 for a detailed exegesis of what has become known as Luther's 'Two Kingdoms' theory of Church and State.

96. Ebeling, p. 180.

97. For such a detailed examination, Cameron's book is a very helpful guide to specific areas of Germany.

98. Hillerbrand, p. 83; see also Rupp, 'Martin Luther', p. 193.

99. Hillerbrand, p. 84.

100. Rupp, 'Martin Luther', p. 194 and Hillerbrand, p. 84.

101. For helpful details, see Cameron, pp. 319-360, and pp. 324-325 on Münster.

102. Hillerbrand, p. 85.

103. Cameron, pp. 402-405.

104. Bainton, *Here I Stand*, p. 224; see his section of this issue, pp. 224-237.

105. Chadwick, pp. 43-44 and Bainton, *Here I Stand*, p. 231.

106. Bainton, *Here I Stand*, p. 230.

107. Ibid., p. 231.

108. Ibid., p. 232.

109. Rupp, p. 194; Bainton, *Here I Stand*, pp. 246-248; Hillerbrand, pp. 84-86.

110. Paul Kennedy, *The Rise and Fall of the Great Powers* (London

and New York, 1987), especially, pp. 31-55, discussing the overstretch of what Kennedy accurately describes as the 'Habsburg bloc'.

111. For fascinating insights into Charles V by a present-day Habsburg and loyal Catholic, see Otto von Habsburg, *Charles V* (London, 1970, English translation; Paris 1967, French original), especially, pp. 82-89 and 149-155.

112. Hillerbrand, p. 86.

113. Bainton, *Here I Stand*, p. 264: Luther goes on to say that children who would not learn it should not eat, servants who declined should be distrusted!

114. For more detail see, for example, Bainton, *Here I Stand*, pp. 248-251, and also FFA/DW, p. 243, for Melanchthon's own struggles.

115. Rupp, 'Martin Luther', p. 195.

116. Bainton, *The Reformation*, p. 149. See the section pp. 149-151.

117. Bainton, *Here I Stand*, p. 254. Technically the Holy Roman Empire continued until abolished in the early nineteenth century. But as the embodiment of a united Christendom, that great medieval ideal which Charles V found so attractive, Bainton is surely correct.

118. Cameron, pp. 267-272, especially, p. 270.

119. Bainton, *Here I Stand*, p. 292.

120. Ibid., pp. 296-298.

121. James I. Packer, 'The Faith of the Protestants' in the *Eerdmans/Lion Handbook*, p. 374.

2

Huldrych Zwingli

1484   birth of Huldrych Zwingli

1506   Zwingli graduates and becomes a parish priest

1516   Zwingli's correspondence with Erasmus thrives

1519   Zwingli made People's Priest of the Great Munster in Zurich

1522   Zwingli resigns his Papal stipend and supports Fast breaking

1523   Zwingli's Sixty Seven Articles; supported by Zurich Councillors in his Biblically based preaching

1529   Colloquy of Marburg: Luther and Zwingli dispute the precise nature and meaning of the Lord's Supper

1529   First war between Protestant and Catholic Swiss Cantons

1531   Renewed fighting: Zwingli is killed in battle

By the Wasserkirche, by the Limmat River, in Zürich, in Switzerland, there is a statue of Huldrych Zwingli, the Swiss Reformer, the subject of this chapter.[1] He holds a Bible in one hand, as one would expect. But in the other hand is a sword: not a symbolic sword to stand for God's word, but the genuine article, to symbolise a very real weapon of warfare.

For this is the paradox of Zwingli. In a century in which thousands died for their faith, it is remarkable that three out of the five subjects of this book – Luther, Calvin and Knox – died peacefully in their beds. Cranmer did not, as we shall see in the chapter on his life. But he died a martyr's death, the victim, like Hus or Tyndale before him, of persecution. Zwingli, by contrast, died in the heat of battle, a warrior's death, and not at all the kind that one would expect for a preacher, a man of God.

Zwingli therefore presents a paradox to us: the proclamation of faith combined with military violence. He was also the one Reformer of these five not to have left a denominational structure behind him – we do not have a 'Zwinglian Church' to go alongside Lutheran, Reformed, Anglican or Church of Scotland churches. Yet one can argue that the *theological* impact Zwingli left behind was enormous. Protestant views on the nature of the Communion Service (or Eucharist) have been divided ever since Luther and Zwingli disagreed over the issue – and the rift remains. Zwingli's ideas were influential in England, as we shall see in the Cranmer chapter. Likewise many have argued that Calvin could never have achieved as much as he did in Geneva and beyond had Zwingli not paved the way for him a generation earlier in Zürich.[2] Lastly, although we have no Baptists in this book, it has

been argued that the Anabaptists whom Zwingli opposed
strongly in his lifetime are his 'illegitimate' theological
descendants.[3] For a man who did not write much, certainly
by comparison with men such as Luther and Calvin, and
who died prematurely in battle, Zwingli left a large legacy.
Having for a while been overlooked and underestimated,
his significance is once again being realised.

When we think of the Swiss Reformation, we usually
tend to think of Calvin and Geneva.[4] This is a double
mistake. Firstly, Calvin was French, not Swiss, and the
Reformation had already been fully underway in that region
for several decades before Calvin was converted to
Protestant Christianity. The key figure in the origins of the
Swiss Reformation was Huldrych Zwingli.

Technically even Zwingli was not Swiss.[5] He was born
in Wildhaus in the Toggenburg, in the province of St. Gall
(or Sankt Gallen in German), an 'Allied District' of the
Swiss Confederation like Geneva, but not an actual part of
it.[6] (Zürich, however, like Basel or Uri were Cantons of
the Confederation itself.) This however is a purely
theoretical distinction, one that lasted until the French
Revolution and the Napoleonic conquest of the area, when
most of the different Cantons and Allied Districts were
united into what is today Switzerland. For all intents and
purposes Zwingli was Swiss, and this is certainly how he
regarded himself.

He was born on the first day of January 1484, the son of
a farmer, or 'free peasant', who was also the local village
magistrate: poor, but not unprivileged. His mother's family
was not without influence: her brother was the Abbot of
Fischingen in Thurgau, and his paternal uncle,
Bartholemaus, while the local priest when Zwingli was

born, went on to become Dean of Wesen, where the young Huldrych later went to school.[7]

From the beginning, Zwingli's biographers have extolled the beauties of the Alps in which he was raised.[8] He himself referred to them in his theological writing, including them as symbols of the power of God's creation, and in one of his translations, of a Psalm, referred to an Alpine meadow. As with those converted through the ministry of the twentieth-century Alpine dweller, Francis Schaeffer, over 400 years later, the mountain scenery had a powerful spiritual, as well as purely aesthetic, effect.[9]

In 1494 young Zwingli found himself studying in Basel, and two years later, in Bern.[10] In the latter, he became interested in the arts, especially in music, and the Dominicans tried to persuade him to enter monastic life. But he was persuaded otherwise by his family, and decided to study theology instead. So in 1498 he went to the famous University of Vienna, then undergoing a period of Reform,[11] and then, four years later, transferred back to Basel, where he graduated in 1506. He did not, significantly, have a doctorate – unlike Luther – and this was to cause his enemies to belittle him as mere 'Master Zwingli' in years to come.[12]

He was strongly influenced by humanism, and, in particular, by a scholastic school named *via antiqua*.[13] Luther, by contrast, trained in the *via moderna* school of thought, and it has been suggested that this divergence in intellectual origins caused some of their later rifts. Humanism, as Alister McGrath has correctly pointed out, did not at this stage necessarily mean anti-Christian, as it has come to mean today.[14] Humanists were those intellectuals seeking to return to the original texts, to

rediscover oratory and the arts. In some areas this meant
going back to the Greek and Latin texts of antiquity. In
biblical studies it meant bypassing the hitherto dominant
Latin translation of the Scriptures, known as the Vulgate,
and going straight back to the original languages in which
the Bible was written. Zwingli therefore studied the New
Testament in its original Greek language, and, along with
other humanists, such as the great Dutch scholar and
thinker, Erasmus, discovered what the Greek text *really*
said.[15] Several mistakes in the Vulgate were discovered,
and the false doctrines that had originated from faulty Latin
translations were thereby exposed. However, as we saw in
the Luther chapter, Erasmus was perhaps wary of bringing
the Bible to a wider, non-scholarly audience. He therefore
tried to discourage Zwingli from taking what was the next
logical step: namely, translating the New Testament from
the more accurate Greek version into the language of the
ordinary people.

Even though Zwingli was a simple parish priest by now,
based from 1506 in the town of Glarus, he was developing
an international reputation.[16] He particularly valued his
correspondence with the great Erasmus[17] – it says much
for Erasmus that he was able to correspond with someone
who was not at one of the leading intellectual centres of
the day.

While it is certainly true to say that Erasmus influenced
Zwingli in the direction of humanism, when it came to
politics and patriotism, the two men were very different.
Erasmus was the archetypal cosmopolitan intellectual, at
home anywhere and everywhere, someone who, while
being Dutch by birth, was very much a citizen of Europe,
an international scholar associated more with the world of

ideas rather than a particular place. Zwingli, however, was a passionate patriot,[18] very Swiss, someone who saw himself as bringing God's word to the Swiss people. Luther, while benefiting enormously from nascent German nationalism and not immune to it himself, arguably was careful not to marry nationalism and faith too closely.

Zwingli, ever the patriot, served with Swiss mercenary troops in their battles ahead.[19] The Swiss were internationally feared as fighters[20] for their own independence, but also for money, for they would sell themselves as soldiers to the highest bidders. (This was still, in essence, the era before the nationally-based professional armies that we know today – the British Gurkha regiments, soldiers from the mountain villages of Nepal who fight in the British Army are one of the last remnants of this older system.)

The Swiss were often victorious, such as their famous victory in 1477, not long before Zwingli's birth, when their troops routed the great Burgundian army of Charles the Bold (the great-grandfather of Holy Roman Emperor Charles V), thereby altering considerably the course of European history. However, in 1515 they in turn suffered an equally devastating defeat, at the Battle of Marignano.[21] Maybe as many as ten thousand Swiss soldiers were killed by French forces, and Zwingli was horrified at the slaughter. While no pacifist, he denounced the Swiss mercenary system.[22] This did not go down too well at Glarus – mercenary revenues were a very major source of income. So in 1516 he moved to the town of Einsiedeln,[23] where his ministry flourished, as did his correspondence with Erasmus.

Zwingli's conversion to a more Protestant or Evangelical way of thinking came around this time as well, in his three years of ministry at Einsiedeln. Here, this process becomes controversial. We normally associate words such as Protestant or evangelical with Luther. Yet Zwingli maintained, and some subsequent historians have supported his claim,[24] that he came to the new way of thinking quite *independently* of Luther. In other words, if true, then Zwingli is as much an originator of the Reformation as Luther, someone whose thought did not so much derive from his Saxon counterpart as arrive on parallel lines at the same destination. Since, however, Luther and Zwingli were to have a major falling out over the issue of Communion, it is by now difficult, this side of the later dispute, to know whether or not such a view can be maintained. It has been argued that Zwingli was not a developed Protestant in public, in his own right, until around 1522,[25] which, chronologically speaking, would put him *after* Luther in terms of public proclamation of Reformation doctrines, whether he came to them independently or as a result of Luther's influence.

However, historians such as Cameron[26] and George[27] are agreed that on the key doctrines, such as justification by faith, Luther and Zwingli were entirely at one, whatever their later disagreements on other issues. In a sense, therefore, it does not really matter whether Zwingli came to possess what we now describe as Protestant theological views on his own, in parallel with but not derived from Luther, or whether Luther in fact had more influence than Zwingli would care to admit.

Zwingli began to preach against popular abuses in the church, and in this he was no different from thinkers such as Erasmus, or the Italian Contarini, who similarly opposed such malpractice but remained within the Catholic fold.

He did, however, break with tradition in attacking indulgences.[28] Unlike with Luther, when Zwingli did so in 1518, the local hierarchy sympathised with him and he even ended up with a Papal stipend.

In 1518, however, his life changed:[29] he was awarded the office of People's Priest at the Great Münster (or Grossmünster) in Zürich, one of the leading cities of the Swiss Confederation. His election, by seventeen votes to seven, was on 11 December 1518, and showed that he was not without opposition. There had been rumours that he had wronged a woman[30] – it should be said that another rival had fathered six illegitimate children! Morality among priests was not high, and in this Zwingli had been no different. He was able to assure them, though, that such unchastity was now over.

He therefore began his ministry at the Great Münster on 1st January 1519, his thirty-fifth birthday.[31]

Zürich, unlike many of the German principalities, but like the German Free Cities, was ruled not by an individual, but by an elected council.[32] Although Swiss independence from the Holy Roman Empire was not officially recognised until the mid-seventeenth century, the Swiss Cantons, of which Zürich was one, were *de facto* entirely independent of Imperial rule. They were, in essence, mini-republics. Decisions were thus made with a greater degree of democratic participation than elsewhere, although they were nowhere as democratic as similar institutions today – Swiss women did not have the vote in national elections until 1971!

But as we saw in the Luther chapter and will see again both here and in the rest of the book, in the sixteenth century the *spiritual was political*. It was secular rulers who made the final decision whether or not the Reformation was accepted. As Euan Cameron has convincingly demonstrated, it was this very fact of *lay* choice,[33] – that ordinary people, through their elected representatives in places such as Zürich, could make such a choice – that was one of the selling features of the Reformation. Without this, Zwingli could not have succeeded in what he was about to do.

Zwingli's Reformation began with preaching, and in a wholly new way. Instead of just going through the set sermons of the traditional lectionary,[34] he ignored precedent and began to preach systematically, verse by verse, through the Gospel of Matthew. This is what we now call *expository* preaching, expounding the plain meaning of the text of Scripture to the listening congregation. Nowadays many of us, especially those from churches with a more Reformed perspective, probably take such sermon-making for granted. But what Zwingli was doing was both new and revolutionary, putting the word of God at the heart of the service, and doing so in a way which explained the Bible to ordinary people. Furthermore, he did so in an applied way, demonstrating the relevance of the passage to the people in the congregation.

In that year Zürich was struck by a major plague, which wiped out a quarter of the city's entire population between August and the beginning of the following year.[35] In September Zwingli himself became a victim and nearly died. His brother did die, one of the two thousand to perish.

Needless to say, the scale of the tragedy affected Zwingli deeply. It has been argued that Zwingli's conversion to the new doctrines was a gradual process[36] – like Luther, and that the enormity of the plague gave him a far more powerful sense of the power and sovereignty of God than he had possessed before. (Zwingli, like Calvin, was a strong believer in the biblical doctrine of predestination,[37] in which God in his mercy and love planned before time to redeem sinners who deserve punishment and thereby predestined them for salvation. The Calvin chapter will explain this in more detail; I mention it here to show that this was a key belief of many at the Reformation, not just, as is often mistakenly held, an aberration of Calvin's own.)

As a result of the many deaths, Zwingli wrote a moving *Plague Song* which some feel shows signs of Zwingli's developing theology.[38] In this *Pestlied* (or *Hymn of Pestilence*) Zwingli wrote:[39]

> Help me, O Lord
> My strength and rock;
> Lo, at the door
> I hear death's knock.
> Uplift thine arm,
> Once pierced for me,
> That conquered death,
> And set me free.

Zwingli, having been spared death became far more aware of the power and presence of God. He therefore went on to write:[40]

> My God! My Lord!
> Healed by Thy hand,
> Upon the earth
> Once more I stand
> Let sin no more
> Rule over me;
> My mouth shall sing
> Alone of Thee.

In 1520 Zwingli resigned his Papal stipend, and in 1522 he formally resigned as the Great Minster's 'People's Priest'.[41] However long it had taken to get there, he had, like Luther, moved into the Reformation camp.[42]

As we have seen (and will continue to throughout this book), the personal/spiritual was political. In Luther's case it was the Elector who protected him; in Zürich, as in all similar city-states and cantons, it was the Town Council. In Zürich this was the large council known as 'The Two Hundred' constituted in 1498, and a Small Council of just fifty people.[43] Both Councils were elected by ordinary lay people, although there was not, as mentioned earlier, anything like the universal suffrage of today. But it was lay power and this was important.

Consequently, it was what we might regard as a trivial event that triggered public acceptance of spiritual change: some pork sausages![44] Some early supporters of the Lutheran cause ate them in Zürich during Lent 1522, in a deliberate breach of Catholic teaching and tradition. Hitherto the civil authorities had backed the church with *civil* penalties for breach of *church* law. Consequently, what to us is a harmless act – eating sausages – became a full-blown political crisis.

Zwingli backed the sausage eaters, in a publication entitled *Concerning Choice and Liberty of Food*.[45] He had kept the fast himself but proclaimed publicly that it was an issue of Christian liberty.[46] Christians do not stand under the law but above it: spiritual obedience is not a matter of keeping external rules but of doing so freely and joyfully.

Since the dispute was now in the open, the City Council decided to follow it up by means of an open dispute – similar to the kind in which Luther had participated. The key here is that it would be a *lay* audience, not clerical, that would take the decision. Secondly, the dispute would be in German, in the vernacular of the laity, rather than in Latin, the language of the clerical élite.[47] As Euan Cameron has convincingly shown, this was a major impetus for the Reformation in general[48] and, as Hans Hillerbrand has commented on this particular issue, '[s]uch a claim to ecclesiastical and theological independence was revolutionary'.[49]

Some six hundred citizens (including the members of The Two Hundred)[50] and all of the local Cantonal clergy gathered together on 29 January 1523 to hear the dispute. The Bishop himself was absent – sending a delegate instead – so it was hardly an even match. Zwingli had prepared *Sixty-seven Articles* as a basis for discussion, but the episcopal representative, John Fabri, refused to recognise them, or indeed the lay assembly, as being valid. (As we saw, Zwingli had a Master's, but not a Doctorate, in theology, giving him lower academic status than those who did.)

The *Articles*[51] laid out clearly two of the essential Reformation themes: the centrality and all-sufficiency of Scripture (*sola scriptura*) and the centrality of Christ's work mediated directly to each believer, or, as Zwingli put it, '[t]hose who assert that the gospel is nothing without the confirmation of the church are in error and blaspheme God.'[52] We saw with Luther that the effect of the Reformation was to undo the penitential cycle upon which the authority of the Church over lay believers was based. Zwingli was now doing the same in Zürich.

He was, however, going further. His superior knowledge of the Scriptures, as Alister McGrath has demonstrated,[53] enabled him to overcome his opponents in debate. But his route to Reformation was, as with Luther, Cranmer and

Calvin, *political*, or, to use the word often used in conjunction with the Reformation, '*magisterial*'.[54] This term, coined by Harvard historian George Williams, describes what Timothy George neatly summarises as 'that pattern of church reform which was officially established and supported by civil authority',[55] if needs be by the 'coercive power of the magistrate'. Zürich has been described as 'the first Protestant state by *magisterial* initiative'.[56] For, as Zwingli himself said when presenting his case before the citizens, 'I say that here in this room is without doubt a Christian assembly; there is no reason why we should not discuss these matters, speak and decide the truth.'[57]

Because Zürich was ruled by a local oligarchy, rather than by a Prince who was himself beholden to the Emperor, the consequence of the political make-up of the town was thus different from Luther's Saxony or of Cranmer's England or Knox's Scotland. The new faith was based upon *sola scriptura* and upon the finished work of Christ upon the cross – or, as Zwingli put it, they would 'try everything by the touchstone of the Gospel and the fire of Paul'.[58]

But it was also very dependent upon the political will of the Council, who, indeed, enforced Protestant teaching with all the vigour with which Catholic doctrines had been enforced hitherto. In 1520 Zwingli had been allowed to continue teaching; now he was specifically mandated by the Council to 'continue, as heretofore, to proclaim the Holy Gospel and the Sacred Scriptures'.[59] The Reformation was now official policy.[60]

The other side of the coin was, as Roland Bainton has made clear, that 'Zwingli's own position came to depend on the Council by which he allowed himself to be re-appointed. . . . Here was a union of church and state even more intimate than in Saxony with the difference that the state was more democratically constituted'.[61] The road to Zwingli's eventual death in battle had unwittingly begun.

By October 1523 Zwingli and the Council were therefore already taking an active role in the new, reformed, liturgy.[62] By 1524, the images had been removed from the churches.[63] But it took until 1525 to get rid of the Mass altogether, once again by City Council decree.[64]

Some of Zwingli's more zealous supporters wanted to take things further still: from them would the future Anabaptists come.[65] Zwingli, like the other four Reformers in this book, did not hesitate to baptise children, seeing baptism much as circumcision had been in Old Testament times.[66] God would sort out later who was and who was not truly elect. Christian faith was still a communal act. For example, the City Council ordered attendance at church on Sunday to be compulsory. However, if, as the Anabaptists came to believe, faith was an act of genuine individual repentance into which one could not, by definition, be born *physically*, then the inherent unity of church and state was thereby overthrown. Anabaptist beliefs in the inevitable and consequential separation of church and state became a *political* threat to the unity of the state, and therefore dangerous.

So while Zwingli rejected the Catholic notion of baptism, seeing it as more 'magical' than scriptural,[67] he stuck to his view of baptism as a covenant act, rather than as a symbol of spiritual rebirth (as Baptists would still hold today). Earlier on, he was more sympathetic to baptistic ideas, but by 1524/5 he had come around to the covenantal idea.

Consequently, when disgruntled followers, such as Felix Manz (sometimes spelled Mantz or Manx), began on 21

January 1525 to practise believers' only baptism, Zwingli opposed them.[68] As he put it in 1527, 'they overturn everything',[69] though, as he recognised, 'even those who are inclined to be critical will say that their lives are excellent'.[70]

Soon, Anabaptists such as Manz himself were being executed for their faith: Protestants put to death not by Catholics but by fellow Protestants.[71] (Indeed, in 1529 at Speyer, both Protestant and Catholic members of the Imperial Diet resolved that Anabaptists should be put to death.[72]) While some Anabaptists did become involved in excesses and strange practices, the vast majority did not. Most in fact, like Menno Simons (after whom the Mennonites are named) became pacifists, so strong was their rejection of the state and all it stood for.[73]

However, it was from followers of Zwingli that the movement began. So while he denounced their views, it was he who had created the environment in Zürich in which they could originate.[74] The loyal Swiss patriot Zwingli would have surely been horrified at the way in which what we now call the Radical Reformation developed. But such is often the way with powerful ideas!

As time went by, Zwingli was himself very much as the 'shepherd' or 'watchman' of his people (to use the epithets which he preferred himself).[75] The position within the Swiss Confederation of Zürich as a *Protestant* Canton in relation to the other still *Catholic* Cantons was a delicate one and continued to remain so.[76] Swiss Cantons continued to go to war with each other over religion as late as the nineteenth century, long after such fratricidal religious wars had ceased elsewhere. Such tensions were just beginning in Zwingli's day and were ultimately to be the cause of his premature death.

Zwingli was also unafraid to propound his own views, even if it meant falling out with his fellow Protestants. On the issue of the Anabaptists, he had the might of the state on his side. But on the issue of Communion the matter was far more complex. For here he was against the progenitor of Reformation himself, Martin Luther. Furthermore, because of the political pressure from Catholic rulers – the Emperor and his allies in Germany, the Catholic Cantons within the Swiss Confederation[77] – the Protestants believed that they should try to present as united a front as possible. One issue prevented that: the nature of Communion.[78]

To both Luther and Zwingli the notion was very simple. The problem was that they regarded their *own* interpretation as obvious – and their opponent's as equally and obviously wrong! Today it seems tragic that these two great men of faith, who agreed so completely on everything else, should let one issue alone divide them.[79] Yet in that disagreement we can see the origins of much of modern Protestantism – we have one Roman Catholic Church and hundreds (if not thousands) of Protestant denominations! *Sola scriptura* is a wonderful thing and a lynchpin of Protestant thought. Yet it goes without saying that once you remove an overarching infallible *church* authority from the equation (as the Catholic Church certainly believed itself to be then, and theoretically still does today), then, even though Protestants all agree on the principle of *sola scriptura*, the fact that no one human authority prescribes *the* correct interpretation of what Scripture is saying means, inevitably, that a whole host of different interpretations of what Scripture is are bound to arise.

Both Zwingli and Luther rediscovered and believed

passionately in *sola scriptura*.[80] Over the issue of believers'
only baptism versus covenant baptism, they agreed with
each other,[81] over and against the radical Anabaptists, who
interpreted scripture in a different way. But over the issue
of the nature of the Communion meal, and the real (or otherwise) presence of Christ, both ended up with completely
different views, each man believing that his own view was
the correct interpretation of scripture.

So while it is a tragedy – especially at a politically critical
juncture early in Reformation history – one can also say
that it was an inevitable consequence of the Protestant
liberation of the laity, the priesthood of all believers, a
doctrine in which both Zwingli and Luther believed.

Likewise it should challenge us to examine our own
attitude towards denominational differences, lest we be
guilty of the error Christ exposes in his parable of the speck
and the beam. We can hardly condemn Luther and Zwingli
for falling out if we condemn fellow Christians in
denominations other than our own! 'You baptise them your
way and I baptise them God's way' may be a good joke,
but it reveals an attitude which we all too often adopt
towards differing views.

It is therefore in an attitude of humility rather than
condemnation that we should approach the great debate
between Luther and Zwingli.

When they met at Marburg in Germany in October 1529,
they came with doctrinal daggers already fully unsheathed.
As George has written, 'the war was on!'[82] Luther published
a book in 1527 against Zwingli entitled *That the Words of
Christ.... Still Stand Firm Against the Fanatics* and Zwingli
rejoined with the book *A Friendly Exegesis...Addressed to
Martin Luther*, a reply so robust in tone that it was deemed

not anything like as amicable as the title suggests.[83]

Agreement on most points – other than Communion, was very nearly reached.

Zwingli had stated his positive views in books such as *Commentary on True and False Religion* and *An Addition or Summary on the Eucharist*, both of which came out in 1526. (Luther's own book, *Confession of Christ's Supper*, came out in 1528.[84])

In essence, to Zwingli, the Communion was a commemoration, a memorial of Christ, whose presence in our lives we commemorate, or remember, whenever we take Communion – or, as Jesus put it when instituting it at the Last Supper, 'do this in remembrance of me'. To Zwingli, Luther, with his view of Christ's physical presence, was in danger of going back to Rome.[85] Zwingli, by contrast, was in Luther's view in danger of going over to the radical fanatics.[86]

Because of the political threat posed by Catholic Princes, the ruler of the Lutheran State of Hesse, Philip the Magnanimous, determined to get Luther and Zwingli together, so that *spiritual* unity could lead to a united all-Protestant *political* alliance. The venue was one of Philip's castles, at Marburg.[87]

Luther's view, when the two titans met at the Marburg Colloquy, was simple. Christ said at the Last Supper: 'This is my body', or in Latin, '*Hoc est corpus meum*.'[88] As a result, said Luther, since Christ himself uttered these words, 'I cannot truthfully pass over them, but must confess and believe that the body of Christ is there.'[89]

To Zwingli, however, Christ did not mean '*is*', but 'signifies'.[90] After all, Jesus also said that he was the 'vine'. He did not mean that he was literally a vine! Likewise, when Paul said in 1 Corinthians 10:4 that 'Christ was that rock', the Apostle was not literally declaring Christ to be made of stone!

Zwingli explained his views more fully by way of analogy. When a merchant leaves home, he gives his wife a ring to remember him by. His ring reminds his wife constantly of his presence while he is away. The husband is not the ring![91] But the husband reminds the wife of himself through the ring and the wife remembers her husband whenever she sees it. So too the Communion: Christ is not physically present in the Communion, but we are reminded of Christ and all he has done for us whenever we celebrate it.

Alister McGrath points out that Paul uses similar analogies in 1 Corinthians 11:23-25 when he quotes Jesus saying that when we celebrate Communion we do so 'in remembrance of me'.[92] Whether one sees this as an analogy or not, though, depends on whether or not one agrees with Zwingli, though McGrath is certainly convincing in his exegesis of both scripture and Zwingli.[93]

The Colloquy at Marburg failed, ultimately, to come to a final conclusion.[94] Melanchthon realised that if Luther permitted Zwingli's position as valid, then any hope of reconciliation with the Catholics would be impossible.[95] Luther's view was bad enough, but Zwingli's interpretation would be beyond the pale.

Meanwhile, Zwingli had not been idle at home. He and others were keen to spread the Reformation to other parts of the Swiss Confederation. Both Zwingli and another leading Swiss Reformer Heinrich Bullinger went to the key Canton of Berne in 1528.[96] There, in the public debate that followed, Zwingli and the posse of reformers with him were victorious. It has been suggested that the event was slightly stage-managed by sheer force of numbers[97] – whether or not one can conclude that, the effect was the same.

The growth of the Reformation in many Cantons within the Federation was of considerable alarm to those parts of Switzerland that had stayed loyal to the Catholic faith, principally those of the ancient 'Forest Cantons' in the centre of the Confederation which had formed the union back in the Middle Ages.[98]

As a result leagues began to be formed on confessional lines, as had been the case with the Holy Roman Empire to the north. Protestant Cantons formed the Christian Civic Union, followed by the Catholic-orientated Christian Union in 1529.[99] Ironically, in view of the fact that the Forest Cantons, such as Uri, had begun partly as rebels against Habsburg rule in medieval times, the Catholic Christian Union obtained help from Charles V's brother, Archduke Ferdinand of Austria, in the form of an agreement to support their defensive alliance.[100]

The failure to get *spiritual* unity at Marburg also meant in practice that the pro-Reformation Swiss Cantons of the Christian Civic Union, including Zwingli's Zürich, did not get the political/military support from the Lutheran Princes in Germany. So when the Christian Civic Union attacked the Christian Union in what has been called an 'offensive defense' [sic][101] in 1529, at a place ten miles south of Zürich called Kappel, they were on their own. Thankfully for them, they were successful, and they imposed upon the Catholic Cantons the First Peace of Kappel on 24 June 1529.[102]

What seems extraordinary to us today is that it was Zwingli himself, a clergyman, a preacher, who had suggested the defensive or preventative attack in the first place! Zwingli's sermons had become increasingly influenced by the Old Testament.[103] Zwingli was keen to see the Christian faith applied in the real world, towards reforming not just the Church, but everything – the whole of society. As he put it, the 'kingdom of Christ is also thoroughly external', as well as within us, internally.[104] The minister and the magistrates were both, equally, the servants of God. This did not just mean war – Zwingli was as keen to help the poor, marginalised and oppressed of society as he was on an aggressive foreign policy. The sacred/secular divide of Western thinking that prevails in our own time simply was not there in Zwingli's day. As he himself put it, 'God's Word will make you pious, God-fearing folks. Thus you will preserve your Fatherland.'[105]

Zwingli, though, did teach that if the state went against the Word of God, it should be resisted. By and large though, the two went very much together – the state could, for example, enforce Christian morality, as it did increasingly in Zwingli's Zürich.

The victory in 1529 had been comparatively bloodless, and the Catholic Cantons were soon breaking the terms of the peace, by persecuting Protestant believers within their jurisdiction. By 1531 Zwingli was outraged, and demanded action.[106] The newly Protestant Berne was hesitant to see conflict, and, as in 1529, urged caution. But they were overruled. In May 1529 economic sanctions were imposed on the Catholic Cantons, in the form of a blockade of imports of wine, iron, salt and grain.[107] Negotiations were tried and failed. Zwingli was for action: he could not abide the innocent suffering of his fellow believers.

The sanctions hurt the Catholic Cantons, and by

September 1531 they were preparing for war (something, it seems, ignored by the citizens of Zürich).[108] In October the Catholic force invaded and the woefully unprepared Zürich army was inadequate to beat off the attack.

Battle was joined on 11 October, once again at Kappel.[109] The Zürich army was overwhelmed and defeated – Zwingli himself was among those killed, along with nine other clergy.[110] The pro-Reformation forces suffered another major military defeat at Gubel on 24 October – in November 1531 they were forced to surrender.[111] The political/military attempts to spread the Reformation had failed, and Zwingli was dead.

Zwingli himself was no more, but his thought lived on. As we shall see, his influence over Cranmer and other English Reformers was great. In Geneva, through Calvin, a French exile, the Swiss were to have a mammoth influence over the subsequent history of the Reformation. So while he failed to prevail at Marburg, and lost his life in battle, his life was far from being in vain. His own motto summarised the way in which he lived: 'Do something bold for God's sake!'[112] He certainly did that, recognising that the *whole* of our life should come under the rule of God. We may differ strongly with some of the means that he chose – civic coercion, and violent conflict – but the principle of total devotion to the cause of Christ is surely one with which we can all agree and by which we can be challenged anew in our own time.

References

1. George, pp. 160-161.

2. As for example does George, p. 159.

3. George, pp. 118-120, 137-138, 140-144 and especially 159.

4. W. P. Stephens, *Zwingli: An Introduction to His Thought* (Oxford, 1992/4) p. vii.

5. A. McGrath, *A Cloud of Witnesses* (Leicester, 1990) pp. 79-80 (henceforth *Cloud*).

6. Ibid.; see also George, p. 108.

7. G. W. Bromiley, 'Zwingli', *Encyclopaedia Britannica, Macropaedia*, vol. 19, 15th edn. (Chicago,1975) p. 1178.

8. George, p. 110; Hillerbrand, p. 53; E. G. Rupp, 'The Reformation in Zürich, Strassburg (sic) and Geneva' in G. R. Elton, ed., *The New Cambridge Modern History*, vol. 2 (Cambridge, 1958) p. 97.

9. See for example *The Tapestry* by his wife Edith Schaeffer.

10. Hillerbrand, p. 53; George, p. 112. The spelling of the name of the city in German is Bern, but in French it is Berne.

11. *Cloud*, p. 80.

12. George, p. 120.

13. Stephens, p. 14; Rupp, p. 98.

14. *Cloud*, pp. 80-81.

15. Ibid.; also George, p. 112; Stephens, pp. 14-15.

16. Hillerbrand, p. 53; Rupp, p. 97.

17. Bromiley, p. 1178.

18. Stephens, p. 13; George, p. 110.

19. Bromiley, p. 1178.

20. George, p. 110.

21. Habsburg, p. 70; Stephens, p. 13; George, p. 110.

22. George, p. 111.

23. Bromiley, p. 1178.

24. See Hillerbrand, pp. 54-55 for a discussion of all the ins and outs. See also Stephens, pp. 1-2, George, p. 113, Cameron, pp. 181-182 and Rupp, p. 99.

25. Stephens, p. 3 and Cameron, pp. 108 and 182-183. As Euan Cameron drolly observes (p. 182), if Zwingli developed his ideas 'entirely independently of Luther, it was the most breathtaking coincidence of the sixteenth century'. George disagrees (p. 113): 'Zwingli's Reformation insights often paralleled Luther's, but did not

derive from them.' Readers will have to make up their own minds.

26. Cameron, pp. 108-110 and 181-182; see also pp. 118-119.

27. George, p. 120.

28. Bromiley, p. 1178.

29. Ibid., p. 1179; Cameron, p. 108.

30. Stephens, p. 16.

31. Rupp, p. 99.

32. Stephens, pp. 7-9; Cameron, p. 108-9. Cameron also states (p. 51) that the self-governing nature, since earlier times, of the Swiss city-states perhaps predisposed them to the Reformation when the time came. See also Hillerbrand, p. 55 and George, p. 115.

33. Cameron, pp. 417-422.

34. George, p. 113; Cameron, p. 108; *Clouds*, p. 83; Rupp, p. 99; Stephens, p. 16.

35. George, p. 113; Stephens, p. 17; Hillerbrand, p. 55.

36. Cameron, pp. 181-182; Stephens, p. 3; George, p. 114.

37. George, pp. 122-126; Stephens, pp. 49-52; Cameron, pp. 128-132.

38. George, p. 114. See also Hillerbrand, p. 55, Stephens, p. 17 and Bromiley, p. 1179.

39. George, p. 114.

40. Ibid., p. 114.

41. Ibid.

42. Cameron, pp. 181 ff.

43. Hillerbrand, p. 54; Stephens, pp. 8-9.

44. Hillerbrand, p. 55; Rupp, p. 100; Cameron, p. 108.

45. Hillerbrand, p. 55.

46. Stephens, p. 18, who argues that this is when Zwingli becomes overtly Evangelical; Bainton, *The Reformation of the Sixteenth Century*, pp. 83-84.

47. George, p. 116.

48. Cameron, pp. 417-422; also Stephens, p. 19.

49. Hillerbrand, p. 55.

50. Hillerbrand, p. 56; George, p. 116.

51. Hillerbrand, p. 56; Bromiley, p. 1179; Rupp, p. 101; Stephens, pp. 19-20.

52. Hillerbrand, p. 56.

53. *Cloud*, p. 84.

54. See George, p. 20 for the conceptual background to this term.

55. Ibid., p. 326.

56. Ibid., p. 117.

57. Ibid., p. 116.

58. Bainton, *The Reformation of the Sixteenth Century*, p. 86.

59. Hillerbrand, p. 56; see also George, pp. 116-117; Cameron, p. 108.

60. *Cloud*, p. 84.

61. Bainton, p. 88.

62. George, p. 118.

63. Hillerbrand, p. 57.

64. George, p. 118; Hillerbrand, p. 57.

65. George, p. 118; Hillerbrand, p. 58.

66. George, pp. 138-141; Stephens, pp. 85-93.

67. George, p. 139.

68. George, p. 137; Stephens, p. 87; Hillerbrand, p. 62.

69. George, p. 143.

70. Bainton, p. 97.

71. Ibid.; George, p. 138; Cameron, pp. 321-322; Ernest Payne, 'The Anabaptists', in G. R. Elton, ed., *New Cambridge Modern History*, Vol. 2, (op. cit.), pp. 120-121.

72. Bainton, p. 102.

73. For an excellent study of the life and thought of Menno Simons, see George, pp. 252-306.

74. George, p. 159 and Hillerbrand, p. 62.

75. George, pp. 118 and 135.

76. Hillerbrand, pp. 92-93; Bromiley, p. 1179.

77. Hillerbrand, p. 93; George, pp. 148-150.

78. George, p. 150.

79. Cameron, p. 165. When Luther and Zwingli met, they agreed on fourteen out of fifteen key principles: Communion was the one upon which they differed. See also George, p. 150 and Bainton, p. 92.

80. Cameron, pp. 137-139.

81. *Cloud*, p. 81.

82. George, p. 149.

83. Cameron, pp. 164-165.

84. Ibid.

85. George, 149.

86. Ibid.

87. Ibid., pp. 149-150; see also Cameron, p. 165.

88. George, p. 150.

89. Ibid., p. 151.

90. All Zwingli quotations in this paragraph come from George, p. 151.

91. *Cloud*, p. 85.

92. Ibid., p.84.

93. Ibid., pp. 84-89.

94. Cameron, p. 165; Stephens, pp. 104-105 and also 78; George, p. 150.

95. Bainton, pp. 92-93.

96. Cameron, pp. 221 and 235-239.

97. Ibid., pp. 238-239.

98. Bromiley, p. 1179; Bainton, p. 90.

99. Cameron, pp. 222-223; Rupp, p. 103; Hillerbrand, pp. 92-93.

100. Stephens, p. 28; Cameron, p. 222; Bainton, p. 90.

101. Bromiley, p. 1179.

102. Rupp, p. 103. Rupp spells Kappel with a 'C', Cappel. (Different historians spell or translate the names in different ways.) Zwingli felt that the Peace was something of a sell-out.

103. George, pp. 135-136.

104. George, pp. 133 and 136. George shows that he disagreed with Luther on this issue.

105. Ibid., p. 111.

106. See Stephens, p. 28.

107. Cameron, p. 223.

108. Ibid.

109. George, p. 158. See also Stephens, p. 29.

110. Ibid.; Stephens, p. 29; Cameron, p. 223.

111. Cameron, p. 223.

112. George, p. 160.

3

John Calvin

1509	Jean Cauvin (= John Calvin) born in France
1523	goes to Paris (and subsequently other cities) to study
1533	Calvin's 'sudden conversion'; has to flee Paris
1534	becomes a Protestant, flees to Switzerland
1536	first of many editions of Calvin's *Institutes* is published (the definitive one being regarded as that of 1559)
1536	Calvin begins his first stay in Geneva
1538	Calvin expelled from Geneva and flees to Strasbourg, where he marries Idelette (who dies in 1549)
1539	Calvin's *Commentary on Romans*
1541	French translation published of his *Institutes*
1541	Calvin returns to Geneva: writes his *Ecclesiastical Ordinances*
1555	Calvin especially active in evangelism of France; gains a sympathetic Council for the first time
1564	Calvin dies

John Calvin is one of the best-known and most controversial of the Reformers. Millions of Christians today, all over the world, are in churches whose theology is described as Calvinist or Reformed, and everyone has heard of Presbyterians of different shades, whose theology also harks back to the life and thought of this sixteenth-century Frenchman.

Calvin thought of himself merely as a 'poor and timid scholar',[1] yet he has either been almost idolised as the greatest Christian since the Early Church, or virtually demonised as a tyrannical ogre who did not hesitate to burn at the stake anyone who dared to disagree with him. There are few historians who are entirely neutral about Calvin, and even in newspapers today, those who know nothing of church history will frequently describe someone who is mean or hard-nosed as having had a 'dour Calvinistic upbringing'.[2] How often are people described as a 'joyous Lutheran' or 'militant Zwinglian'? I have never seen such monikers attached to personalities today. Calvin stands alone in this regard.

So before we look at Calvin, we need to consider: why all the hatred? Time and again, for example, people bring up the execution of Servetus (at which we will look in more detail later), not just to condemn Calvin for brutality (of which he was actually entirely innocent), but as the justification for rejecting his entire thought.[3] 'You can't believe Calvin,' they say in effect. 'Look at what he did to Servetus.'

Furthermore, with no other Reformer does this happen. We saw in the chapter on Luther that he was in favour of a princely policy of slaughtering *thousands* of rebellious peasants. He favoured the savage persecution of

Anabaptists, whom he denounced ferociously and, as we also saw, he was arguably anti-Semitic as well, granting twentieth-century German anti-Semites in the Nazi period a twisted theological rationale for the Holocaust. As for Zwingli, he died not in bed, but in battle.

Yet we do not reject Luther's view of *sola fidei* because of his approval of princely slaughter, nor do we reject *sola scriptura* because of his coarse language or views of the Jews. Our view of the Communion Service (was Luther or Zwingli correct?) does not depend on our view of Zwingli's propensity to wield the sword in defence of his views. With Calvin however, the execution of just one man in an age when thousands of people were slaughtered by *both* sides (a fact which Protestants often forget: we are as guilty as the Catholics), it seems odd to single him out as being guilty and to discredit his entire *corpus* of thought on the basis of a single, and usually much exaggerated, accusation.

It seems to me that there are several reasons why many are not attracted to the teachings of Calvin. Firstly, there is the mammoth nature of Calvin's thought. People who reject him and his thought want an excuse, and the myth of his supposed tyranny in Geneva, of which he was never even a full citizen, provide such critics with a golden excuse, even though they are thereby forced to be inconsistent and overlook the many failings of other Reformers.

Secondly, we need to remember that it is the message we are looking at, rather than the messenger. We have a wonderfully human, but ultimately erroneous, habit of reacting to what we hear on the basis of our reaction to the speaker. A winsome personality wins more adherents than someone dour, even if it is the dour person who is telling us the truth. Someone like Luther is a larger than life, warts and all personality, to whom we can more easily relate. Calvin, by contrast, was by temperament a more introvert figure, far less easy to get to know and therefore less attractive to the mindset of today.

Thirdly, Calvin was very much a man of the second generation of the Reformers: he was only eight years old when Luther nailed his theses to the Wittenberg door. Consequently, he was a consolidator, not a trailblazer, and this too, somewhat inevitably, gives him a less heroic stature in the eyes of many.

We know a lot about Luther's thoughts and feelings because Luther himself told us about them. As Alister McGrath has written:

> [A] curious silence resonates through history concerning the personality of Calvin. Of the intellectual stimulus he injected into the history of ideas we know much, yet of the historical person who generated them we know tantalisingly little. As a human being, Calvin remains an enigma.[4]

Yet Calvin's *ideas* have had a massive impact, and not just upon the Church. As we shall discover, there are those who have argued that modern capitalism, if not capitalism itself, originated from the outworking of Calvin's theology. Calvin's English-speaking followers, the Puritans, played a major role in the establishment of America, and since the USA is the most prosperous and powerful single nation upon earth, Calvin, through his later disciples, has thereby played a critical role in shaping the world in which we live today.

So although Calvin in and of himself remains a bit of a mystery to us, we cannot, in another sense, understand life at the end of the twentieth century without a proper comprehension of Calvin and his thought.

Early years

Although we naturally associate Calvin with Geneva and Switzerland (of which Geneva has been a part since 1815, long after Calvin's death in 1564), he was, in fact, French. He was born in the French town of Noyon, the son of Gerard Cauvin, a lawyer of humble origins, who worked his way up to a responsible position on the legal side of the Cathedral at Noyon. Jeanne, his mother, was the daughter of an innkeeper from the French town of Cambrai. The man we know today as John Calvin was born on 10 July 1509 and spent his early years as Jean Cauvin. Calvin is the Anglicisation of his Latin name, *Calvinus*.

When we look at Calvin's early years, 'we are confronted with a near-total absence of material from his own pen relating to his formative period.'[5] So much of what Calvin thought, how he developed, grew up, felt, and more besides, remains a closed book to us. Speculation might help, but with a character as controversial as Calvin, it is important to remember that any speculation you read probably reveals far more about the writer than about Calvin himself! What we do know is that, like C. S. Lewis in our own century, Calvin lost his mother when he was very young – in his case, aged five or six. If Calvin was by nature an introvert, such a shock must have rendered him more inward-looking still.

In May 1521, Calvin received a titular benefice. This meant that he had the job and the salary while someone less fortunate did all the work – the kind of clerical abuse against which Luther and the German Reformers were beginning to protest. The positive outcome was that Calvin's education was paid for.

In 1523, Calvin went to Paris to study, one of the great intellectual centres of Europe since the Middle Ages, and still today (thus a contrast with the comparatively backwater and recently founded University of Wittenberg).

Hitherto scholars have presumed that Calvin went first to the Collège de la Marche at the University.[6] This has now been shown by Alister McGrath to be wrong.[7] What everyone agrees upon, though, is that he was soon at the Collège de Montaigu, another of the constituent parts of the University (of which the Collège de Sorbonne is the most famous). Here Calvin was lectured to by some of the finest scholars in Europe, whose knowledge of scholastic theology and of Hellenist literature was probably unsurpassed.

Luther set out to be a lawyer but became a theologian. Calvin, by contrast, began with the study of theology and ended up being trained as a lawyer.[8] Having received his Master of Arts degree from Paris he transferred, at his father's wish, to study law at the University of Orléans, beginning there in March 1528. Once more, his lecturers were of international calibre. One of them, the Italian jurist Andrea Alciati, was based at Bourges, and Calvin transferred there in 1529. At Bourges was the classical scholar Melchior Wolmar, of Lutheran sympathies, who taught Calvin Greek, and whom Calvin was later on to summon to Geneva to teach Greek there instead.

In May 1531, Gerard Cauvin died, and young Calvin, still only 21, had to curtail his studies. He decided to return to Paris, to study both Greek and Hebrew. There he published, in 1532, his first work, a commentary on the

classical Latin scholar Seneca's book, *On Clemency* (*De
Clementia*). At this point in his life, Calvin looked far more
set to be an eminent classicist in the European humanist
tradition than the eminent Protestant Reformer he was to
become. Soon after the book's publication, he returned to
Orléans to gain his doctorate, and by October 1533 he was
back in Paris again. Humanists were very much in favour
at the royal court of Emperor Charles V's great enemy,
King Francis I, and worldly success for Calvin beckoned.

All this was changed by what Calvin, at a later date,
referred to as his 'sudden' conversion.[9] Scholars have
debated when exactly this happened: as so often with
Calvin, we do not know, and, indeed, it is not clear whether
'sudden' means precisely that, or whether it was a major
turning point of sudden realisation at the end of a long
period of reflection. His one reference to this event was
written in the preface of his *Commentary on the Psalms* in
1557: as with Luther's experience in the tower, it was
therefore composed many years after the event. He wrote:

> At last, God turned my course in a different direction by the
> hidden bridle of his providence.... By a sudden conversion
> to docility, he tamed a mind too stubborn for its years.[10]

While 'debates have raged over the exact meaning and
date of Calvin's "conversion",'[11] the one thing upon which
we can agree is that it was momentous and lasting. Another
thing that we can say too is that it was profoundly risky:
the King of France was no friend of Protestants. There was,
in Calvin's life, no Frederick the Wise.

Calvin now, in fact, had to flee France for his life,
because of the sermon preached on All Saints Day (1

November 1533) by Nicholas Cop, his distinguished University colleague. By all accounts Cop far exceeded the safe Erasmian criticisms of the Church – strong Lutheran undertones were to be found as well. It used to be thought that Calvin played a part in writing Cop's sermon. Some scholars now deny this happened, others affirm the traditional story.[12] The thing upon which people unite is that Calvin, being close to Cop, had to flee too, possibly by escaping with bed sheets from his room while the authorities were banging on the door![13]

Calvin was briefly, in 1534, able to re-enter France for a while, spending some time with friends in the city of Angouleme. In May 1534, he made his official break with the Catholic Church by resigning his benefices at Noyon Cathedral.

Being a Protestant was now dangerous – some Lutheran supporters in Paris had posted pro-Luther placards, and this enraged the King. As Cameron writes, with the path back to the Church gone, then 'no doubt, his decision to come down firmly on the protestant side did feel like a 'sudden' providential change'.[14]

Calvin initially headed for Basel, the Swiss town where many Reformers had found refuge. Switzerland at the time was a confederation of city-states, as we have seen from the chapter on Zwingli. Cop was there already, as was the dying Erasmus himself, who died in June 1536, still a critic of the abuses of Catholicism but ultimately loyal to it unto death.

The *Institutes*

Here Calvin began the epic work which was to ensure him world-wide and lasting fame: the *Institutes of the Christian*

Religion. (For details of all the many editions in different languages, see McGrath's life of Calvin.[15]) It was finished in 1535, and finally published in Latin in 1536. The first edition was much smaller than the mammoth later editions (especially the definitive edition of 1559 – Calvin was to rewrite and rewrite it many times!)

It was dedicated to King Francis I. Francis had, for political reasons, allied himself to the German Lutherans, the political opponents of Charles V, Francis' long-time rival. (For similar reasons, the French were to support the Protestant side in the Thirty Years War of 1618-1648: the enemy of their Habsburg rivals was their friend.) Francis had to justify his persecution of French Protestants by regarding them as Anabaptists, a group who, as we saw in the Luther chapter, gained the hatred of Luther and the Protestant princes as well as of the Catholics.

Calvin and the bulk of French Protestants were not Anabaptists, and the accusation disgusted Calvin. He denied the charge and did all he could to clear the good name of his fellow French Protestants.[16] In the *Institutes* he tried to demonstrate the orthodoxy of their beliefs.

The full title of the book explains the basic themes: 'The basic teaching of the Christian religion comprising almost the whole sum of godliness, and whatever is necessary to know on the doctrine of salvation.' The book had six parts: on the Ten Commandments, the Apostle's Creed, the Lord's Prayer and the two sacraments (Calvin agreeing with Luther that these consisted only of baptism and communion), with a chapter against what Calvin deemed to be false sacraments and a final chapter on Christian liberty, church power and civil power.[17] The book, initially anonymous, was a major best-seller, propelling its shy author into an up and coming theologian of international importance.

Calvin's aim was to teach people how 'God's glory may be kept safe on earth...how Christ's Kingdom may be kept in good repair among us'.[18]

Why was it such a success? Others had tried to make summaries of basic Protestant belief, but perhaps Timothy George is right when he says that 'all in all, Calvin presented more clearly and more masterfully than anyone before him the essential elements of Protestant theology'.[19]

As Alister McGrath correctly comments:

> The originality, power and influence of Calvin's religious ideas forbid us to speak of him merely as a 'theologian' – though that he certainly was – in much the same way as it is inadequate to refer to Lenin as a mere political theorist. Through his remarkable ability to master languages, media and ideas, his insights into the importance of organization and social structures, and his intuitive grasp of the religious needs and possibilities of his era, Calvin was able to forge an alliance between religious thought and action which made Calvinism a wonder of its age.[20]

This is what one must, I think, grasp about Calvin: he was a superb *systematiser*, a teacher who, by the genius with which he put complex ideas together, was able to transform the minds, and therefore the lives, of countless thousands of people in his own lifetime and, as we now know, millions since. We do not live in a mere vacuum. All of us have basic ideas by which we live. Calvin's aim was to show how we could have 'business with God'.[21] Calvin's theology was in itself not in a vacuum, but in a relationship with a real God who is there and cares for us.

His aim was for his book to 'be a key to open a way for all
children of God into a good and right understanding of
Holy Scripture'.[22] Calvin did not invent his views: he
expounded what he believed to be the clear message of
God's word to us, the Bible.

To that extent, he was *not* a systematiser, but an
expositor: as his twentieth-century follower, Martyn Lloyd-
Jones, once told me, we must be 'Bible Calvinists, not
system Calvinists'.[23] We can all too easily get sucked into
what we feel is a neat system of thought, and forget that
we ought to make everything that we believe compatible
with Scripture, even if that means jettisoning ideas that
flow well in a purely logical sense but are nonetheless
incompatible with what the Bible teaches. Although Calvin
did not make that mistake himself, it is arguable that many
of his followers have done so over the ensuing centuries –
and I include myself, as a Calvinist, in that caution!
Likewise we must be careful (a) to make sure that Calvin
actually said it, rather than some later follower ascribing
his own views to the great man, to give them credence and
(b), far more important, to do what Calvin and the other
Reformers would all have done (and urged us to do),
namely to test all views against God's word, the Bible.
Those who give their hero the authority that belongs to
Scripture alone are doing their hero no favours! Perhaps
because I am a Calvinist myself, I am aware that Calvinists
are especially guilty here, and it is even possible that one
of the reasons why Calvin is so controversial a figure even
today, at the beginning of the twenty-first century, is that
some of his present-day followers are enough to put anyone
off taking his views seriously!

In Basel, Calvin was beginning a life of exile that was

to become familiar to many of the early Protestants (and, as we should not forget, to many Catholics excluded from the growing number of Protestant countries).

Comes to Geneva

Calvin then visited the Italian duchy of Ferrara (Italy itself did not exist until the 1860s), to try to establish the Reformation there. He had originally intended to go back to Basel or to Strasbourg (now a French city but then a border city between France and the Holy Roman Empire), where there was also a growing number of Protestants. However, the semi-continuous state of warfare between King Francis I and Emperor Charles V meant that the direct route was physically unsafe. So, in August 1536, he found himself in the city-state of Geneva, the city with which he has become synonymous.

Geneva was a city-state slowly becoming independent of the Dukes of Savoy (the dynasty which was instrumental in uniting Italy in the nineteenth century).[24] It was allied to the growing Swiss Confederation, but did not actually join it until 1815 – so while we refer to Geneva at this time as Swiss (for sake of convenience), we are technically incorrect.

Far more important so far as Calvin was concerned is that Geneva had just started to turn towards the Protestant faith: on 26 May 1536, the Genevans had voted to 'live henceforth according to the law of the gospel and the Word of God, and to abolish all papal abuses'.[25]

The turning of city-states such as Geneva to Reformed or Protestant faith was therefore very different from the situation in the princely states, both in the Holy Roman Empire, or beyond, such as England or the Scandinavian kingdoms.[26] It was the citizens who made the decisions.

Furthermore, in Geneva itself, the inhabitants were divided into three categories: *citizens* who were born and baptised within the city to citizen parents; *bourgeois* who were able to obtain a kind of second-class citizenship; and *inhabitants* (*habitants*) who were, in effect, legal resident aliens with no privileges.[27] Only full *citizens* (*citoyens*) could vote for or be part of the *Petit Conseil* or ultimate ruling body.

Calvin has been misrepresented, as we have seen, as a tyrant and ogre. It is vital to remember that until 1559, fully twenty-three years after he first came to Geneva, he was merely a *habitant* with no vote or privilege of any kind. Not until 1559 did he become a *citizen*, and then only as a b*ourgeois*. Being born an outsider, a foreigner in France, he was never a full *citoyen*, nor, indeed, could he ever, by definition, have become one. We must always keep this in mind as we study the sometimes tempestuous relationship between Calvin and the city in which his presence became famous.

Calvin did not intend to stay in Geneva long. However, when the Reformer Guillaume Farel, who was already in the city, heard that Calvin was there, he came to see him and in no uncertain terms urged him to stay and help consolidate the growth of Protestantism there.

Farel, 'burning with a wondrous zeal to advance the Gospel, suddenly set all his efforts at keeping' Calvin in Geneva, Calvin tells us, continuing,

> After having heard that I was determined to pursue my own private studies – when he realised that he would get nowhere by pleas – he came to the point of a curse: that it would please God to curse my leisure and the quiet for my studies that I was seeking, if in such a grave emergency I should

withdraw and refuse to give aid and help. This word so overwhelmed me that I desisted from the journey I had undertaken.[28]

Farel's threatened curse worked: Calvin stayed!

Calvin began a series of unpaid lectures at the Church of St. Pierre in the autumn of 1536, and was later elected the church's pastor.

However, it is worth remembering here that Calvin's position initially depended upon Farel's own position in relation to the Genevan authorities, and that the latter position was rather shaky, dependent in turn on the vagaries of Genevan city politics. Calvin was simply known as 'that Frenchman'.[29]

The anti-Savoy party on the Council were linked to the Swiss city of Berne, and it was this group which especially wished to evangelicalize the city. Here Calvin became active as an official spokesman in the public debate which took place in October 1536. (Cameron makes clear that the *public* disputation of doctrine, and the fact that local citizens made the decision rather than having it imposed by the clergy, was a key factor in popularising the cause of the Reformation.[30]) Calvin's intervention on 5th October proved decisive, and, as McGrath aptly comments: 'The dramatic effect of this intervention was considerable, and gave the evangelical side an even greater advantage than that which they already enjoyed.'[31]

Calvin then set about producing a decent *Instruction in Faith* as a means of educating ordinary Genevans in the basic rudiments of the Reformed faith. It had emerged that Calvin was the hitherto unknown author of the *Institutes*: this, plus Calvin's stout defence of biblical Christianity, was establishing him as a front rank defender of the new doctrines of the Reformation.

Unfortunately for Calvin, his position still relied, despite his growing reputation, on the ins and outs of Genevan city council politics. The party behind Calvin and Farel, having done well in the 1537 elections, lost control in 1538. Much of the debate was not so much on doctrine itself, but on the extent to which Geneva should follow the wishes of her powerful Swiss protector, the city of Berne, which was adopting a cautious policy on the issue of church rites.

In April 1538, Calvin and Farel were expelled from Geneva. It looked as if his link with the city, and the attempts that he, Farel and others were making to turn Geneva into a truly Reformed city, were over.

Moves to Strasbourg

Calvin ended up, as he had perhaps originally intended, in Strasbourg, which as Timothy George has commented, 'were undoubtedly the happiest years of his life'.[32]

Here he was alongside the great German Reformer, Martin Bucer. Calvin looked after the French-speaking exiles' church. He also got married, to a widow named Idelette de Bure. Calvin was no cold-blooded man when it came to married life: he described Idelette as 'the excellent companion of my life'.[33] However, he had firm views on what a wife should be like, writing to Farel:

> I am not of the wild race of lovers who, at the first sight of a fine figure, embrace all the faults of their beloved. This is the only beauty which allures me, if she is chaste, if not too nice or fastidious, if economical, if patient, if there is hope that she will be interested about my health.[34]

Sadly, their one child, Jacques, died young and Idelette herself died in 1549, leaving Calvin very much the grieving widower. Calvin was surrounded by children for most of his life though: his stepchildren through Idelette, and his eight nephews and nieces, all of whom lived at their uncle's house in Geneva. As one biographer has written, Calvin's great theological works were composed 'not.... in an ivory tower, but against the background of teething troubles'.[35]

Calvin, being both a hypochondriac and an acute introvert, was deprived at a critical time of someone who could have soothed his anxieties and brought him out of himself. This is something that we should not forget when we think of Calvin: a lonely man deprived of his greatest and closest human companions, his wife and son.

In his absence, Geneva had gone through both religious and political upheaval, including an attempt, by Cardinal Jacopo Sadoleto to restore Catholicism. (Calvin's rebuttal to Sadoleto has been called 'the finest brief apology for the Reformation ever written'[36] and 'a literary *tour de force*, perhaps the best apology for the Reformed faith written in the sixteenth century'.[37])

Some have seen Calvin's correspondence with Sadoleto as a 'bridge building exercise'.[38] Certainly, if one looks at the actual wording of the rather irenic correspondence, a good case can be made for this. Sadoleto agreed with Calvin on the basic Reformation tenet that we 'obtain salvation by faith alone.... When we say that we...hold that in that very faith love is comprehended'.[39] They disagreed on whether the Reformers were innovative or traditional, Calvin asserting that 'all we have attempted has been to renew the ancient form of the Church'.[40]

One does wonder, though, how typical Sadoleto was as

a representative of his church. Certainly, there were like-minded Cardinals, such as Contarini, who similarly sympathised with the doctrine of justification by faith. The distinguished Oxford historian, Felipe Fernandez-Armesto, writing with Derek Wilson, points out that while the Council of Trent abhorred Protestants, the actual wording of one of the decrees does allow for justification by faith of a kind.[41]

However, as Euan Cameron points out, such moderate voices as Contarini's tended to be overruled – in his case as early as 1541.[42] Indeed, as Cameron also shows, the Catholic moderates ended up being squeezed out by the younger generation of more hard-line Catholics, with those moderates who were open to early Reformed doctrine, such as Vermigli (better known to us as Peter Martyr), going over fully to the Protestant side.[43]

It is tragic that so much violence took place as a result of the Reformation, and that calmer voices were ignored. But such, alas, was the climate of the times.

Calvin was not idle when in Strasbourg: a French edition of the *Institutes* came out in 1541, and in 1539, not long after his arrival, he published his masterful *Commentary on Romans*, a book, like many others of his works, still in print today, over 450 years later. On top of all this, Calvin also found time to write a highly influential book on liturgy: *The Form of Ecclesiastical Prayers and Hymns*. He, lastly, wrote a book on the vexed issue of communion rites – the *Little Treatise on the Holy Supper*, in which he tried carefully to steer a middle way between the increasingly hardening positions of the Lutherans and the Zwinglians.

Timothy George has commented:

Had Calvin died in 1541 at the ripe age of thirty-two, he would still be revered today as one of the greatest theologians and one of the ablest writers among the reformers.[44]

Returns to Geneva

However, that year, he did not die but returned to the maelstrom of Geneva. Calvin was not at all happy with the prospect, referring to Geneva as a 'gulf and whirlpool'.[45] He returned, very reluctantly, on 13 September 1541.

He presented the City Council with his idea of what a church should be like: his *Ecclesiastical Ordinances*, a work which, whatever the difficulties he had in instituting them successfully and permanently in Geneva, was to have an enormous effect on Reformed Churches world-wide thereafter, right down to the present day. There were to be four types of church officer: pastors, teachers (called doctors at the time), elders and deacons, to look after, respectively, the doctrine, education, discipline and welfare of the Church. Equally vital within the church was the Consistory, made up of the elders and pastors.

The Genevans approved the ideas – in theory. Calvin was now back to stay, but it was to be at least fourteen years before his position there was to be at all secure, a fact all too often forgotten by hostile historians. As Alister McGrath so properly points out, the 'myth of the "great dictator of Geneva"...where this myth is not a total invention, it is a serious distortion of the historical facts',[46] not least because, as we have seen, Calvin was never even a full citizen of Geneva, let alone its dictator. Geneva was a democracy of its native-born citizens and it was *they*, frequently to Calvin's immense frustration, who took all the key decisions, and never the French foreigner living in their midst. If they did what Calvin wanted it was only because he had persuaded them, often after long debate, rather than because they were under some mythical kind of Calvinist dictatorship.

The main thing about the *Ecclesiastical Ordinances* is that they were designed for churches in all kinds of *political* conditions, including that of vicious persecution.[47] This meant that they could be implemented both in Geneva, where there was a pro-Reformation city council, and in France, where the French Protestants (known increasingly as *Huguenots*) were subject to sporadic and often quite violent state persecution by the authorities. This gave Calvinist-influenced churches a powerful sense of internal self-discipline which was to stand them in good stead. While French Protestantism eventually withered over time to a small minority, Calvin's English-speaking followers, the Puritans, had a mammoth effect which is still felt worldwide today.

Calvin spent much of the time between his return in 1541 and his final political consolidation in 1555 trying to ensure that the institutions which he had set up were effective.

One of these was the Consistory, which came into being in 1542.[48] It consisted of members of the Venerable Company of Pastors (of which Calvin was Moderator), which had nine members in 1542 and sixteen by Calvin's death in 1564, along with twelve lay elders elected by the magistrates of the city. Its aim was to keep an eye on not just the spiritual but also on the moral welfare of the citizens of Geneva. Here it acquired in the eyes of some a rather stern reputation,[49] made jocular in those of others: one woman, when told that her dress was immodest, said that if people thought so, they could look the other way![50]

It is important to remember that the most severe power the Consistory had was that of excommunication, or expulsion from the church. Powers such as execution or imprisonment were beyond them. As the City Council made very clear:

> [A]ll this is to take place in such a manner that the ministers have no civil jurisdiction, nor use anything but the spiritual sword of the Word of God. . . . nor is the Consistory to detract from the authority of the *Seigneurie* or ordinary justice. Civil power is to remain unimpeded.[51]

The rulers, or *seigneurs*, of the City Council were firmly in control.

Michael Servetus

This is all vital to remember when we come to 1553 and the trial of Michael Servetus (born in Spain as Miguel Serveto), whose burning at the stake is all too often invoked unfairly to blacken Calvin's reputation and, as we saw, to deny his theological teaching as well.[52]

We need to look at who Servetus was. He was not simply someone who denied the Trinity, but he also held views which Calvin felt to be even more repugnant.[53] For example, he wrote:

> that man is able to put off mortality and be clothed in immortality only if he first put off humanity and acquire divinity through union with the divine man, the Son of the eternal God.[54]

The anti-Trinitarians in general were completely different from the other groups in the radical reformation, the Anabaptists and the Spiritualists.[55] These last two groups were orthodox in *theology*: it was *church* doctrines, such as the baptism of believers only, or the separation of Church and State, where they differed from the mainstream. Anti-Trinitarians, of whom Servetus was one, went far further and denied some of the core doctrines of faith upon which Calvinists, Lutherans, Anabaptists and Catholics were agreed.

One therefore comes to the story of Servetus' execution in Geneva. Servetus was fortunate to be still alive when he got to Geneva in 1553. He had been condemned for heresy in Lyon in France (after 1551 lower courts were free to execute heretics at will) and the authorities there had to be satisfied with burning Servetus by effigy instead.

The situation in France was getting very severe for heretics: thirty-nine people were burned at the stake for heresy in Paris alone between May 1547 and May 1550[56] (not to mention the numerous Anabaptists slaughtered in Germany by Lutheran and Catholic alike).

It is vital to remember that 'the trial, condemnation and execution (including the selection of the particular mode of execution) of Servetus were mainly the work of the city council, at a period in its history when it was particularly hostile to Calvin'.[57]

So when we look at Servetus, we can but conclude that Calvin was someone of his time; Protestants and Catholics alike believed in the execution of heretics.[58] Not only that, but in an age in which *thousands* were executed for their view of theology, the fact that Servetus was the *only* person executed for heresy in Geneva in Calvin's time in fact shows Geneva, if not indeed Calvin himself, was *more* tolerant, rather than less, than the vast majority of Christian cities or states of this time. In an age of mass execution, the *single* execution of Servetus, in which Calvin, as a non-citizen, played a tangential rather than central part, perhaps shows us much about the mercy of the man (or at least of the Geneva City Council) rather than his much vaunted but seriously over-rated wrath. Calvin, some argue, advised the prosecution, rather than being the main prosecutor himself.

Perhaps one of the reasons for the virulence of the opposition to Calvin today is his doctrine of predestination. People in many circles widely dislike the concept, and so they latch on to the Servetus episode and use it as an excuse to discredit Calvin and thus the doctrine associated with his name.

This is puzzling: predestination is certainly not something invented by Calvin, as we shall see – St. Augustine certainly believed in it, and both Augustine and Calvin believed in it because they believed it to be taught by Scripture. Furthermore, it is evident that Luther himself believed in it – he wrote as early as 1517, 'The perfectly infallible preparation for grace, the one and only valid attitude, is the eternal election and predestination of God.'[59]

Does one reject predestination because of Luther's attitude to repressing rebellious peasants and Anabaptists? I have never heard of such a dual criticism! Yet with Calvin, predestination and Servetus seem frequently linked.[60]

One thing, though, is for sure – on the facts of the Servetus case, one cannot bring a case against Calvin of the kind desired by the opponents of the doctrine of predestination. Maybe it would be better for such critics to do what we should all do, and attack the doctrine purely on its merits, and on the grounds of the strengths and weaknesses of Calvin's (and Augustine's, Luther's and that of countless others, such as Jonathan Edwards and George

Whitefield) biblical exposition. If we *really* believe in the Reformation doctrine of *sola scriptura*, we should look at doctrines on *scriptural* grounds rather than in terms of *ad hominem* attacks on later expositors. After all, if we are *truly* Protestant, we should argue on scripture and not on tradition! (The same applies equally to modern Calvinists, who are as guilty here as their Arminian opponents.)

In any case, the real energies of Calvin during this period were not primarily engaged in the negative side of heresy hunting, but in the positive desire to see the evangelisation of his native France. Geneva was the centre for a massive campaign of evangelism designed to bring the doctrines of the Reformation to a nominally Catholic France.

Scores of French exiles were trained as pastors in Geneva and the surrounding countryside and sent as missionaries back into France. (It is significant that their goal was setting up churches and becoming pastors of the newly formed resultant congregations: evangelism then, unlike much of it today, was resolutely *church* based.) This was very dangerous for the new pastors and their congregations – not until 1562 was any kind of Protestantism (especially of the Calvinist variety) tolerated, which meant that all such activity was illegal.[61] From 1555 onwards the evangelistic move was especially powerful, though the City Council had to make it clear to a hostile French Government that it was the churches who were behind the programme as opposed to the City Council itself. By 1562, when limited toleration appeared, there were 1785 consistories in France. The middle class was especially open, and some (but not all) of the aristocracy; only the peasantry remained overwhelmingly Catholic.

Tragically, in France as in Germany, the spiritual

became political, and led to what has been called the French Wars of Religion, which lasted effectively until 1598. This, though, was mostly after Calvin's death – he was spared the horrors of war in his native land. It took yet longer still for the spiritual and political to be decoupled, notably of course, in the strongly Calvinist/Puritan-influenced United States of America. But that is a story beyond the scope of this book.

By 1555, Calvin finally had a Council sympathetic to what he was trying to do. In 1559 he was able to set up an Academy, the genesis of the future University of Geneva, and Reformed-minded Christians from all over Europe came to study and live in the city. (This included many from England, fleeing the persecution of Queen Mary I between 1553 and 1558. The Genevan Exiles, as they were known, were to have a major influence in the reign of her successor, Elizabeth I, and in the subsequent development of English, and later American, Puritanism.) Calvin thereby acquired a huge international influence, in Scotland as we shall see in the later chapter on John Knox, and also in the northern part of what was then the Spanish Netherlands. Scottish, German and Dutch Calvinism was in turn not just to shape those areas but also, through subsequent emigration, the nascent American colonies. Thus one of the most powerful of international spiritual movements of our own times was born. Calvinism was international in a way that has not been so true of Lutheranism and Anglicanism.

Calvin's time of major influence in Geneva (during which, as we have seen, he was still only a *bourgeois*, not a full citizen) lasted only nine years. By the 1560s, his health, which was never truly robust, began to decline. He died on 27th May 1564.

Predestination

Space does not permit too great or detailed a critique of Calvin's thought – and, in any case, the secondary material on his theology, both friendly and hostile, is enormous! What I will do here, therefore, is to look at his most contentious view – predestination – by putting it in its proper place in his overall scheme. I will then examine briefly the other thing which is widely attributed to Calvin's influence: the Protestant work ethic and the rise of modern capitalism.

In his *Institutes* of 1559, Calvin wrote:

> We call predestination God's eternal decree, by which he compacted with himself what he willed to become of each man. For all are not created in equal condition; rather, eternal life is foreordained for some, eternal damnation for others. Therefore, as any man has been created to one or other of these ends, we speak of him as predestined to life or death.[62]

Two things are essential to an understanding of Calvin's doctrine here: (a) Calvin did not invent the doctrine – indeed Luther and Zwingli had said it all before him, and others for centuries before that; and (b) it was by no means central to his doctrinal scheme, although a key part of it.

As Timothy George writes:

> He certainly did not set out to organize his entire theological program around this idea.... For Calvin predestination was from first to last a pastoral concern. For the believer the fact of election is an ex post facto reflection on how, amid the darkness and death of sin, God's grace has broken through.[63]

In fact, predestination does not enter the definitive 1559 edition of the *Institutes* until the end of volume three!

Providence as such comes in volume one, under God the Father, predestination appears in the discussion of the work of the Holy Spirit in the third volume. Furthermore, as we have seen, the doctrine certainly did not prevent Calvin from being profoundly active in evangelism, something that was to be equally true of later followers, such as George Whitefield and Jonathan Edwards in the eighteenth century, Spurgeon in the nineteenth, and Martyn Lloyd-Jones in the twentieth.[64]

Predestination, therefore, is primarily a doctrine of pastoral comfort: those who are truly redeemed do not need endlessly to fret about whether they are saved or not. Bainton has commented on the great strength this gave to Calvinists:

> For Calvin the doctrine of election was an unspeakable comfort because it eliminated all such worries and freed man from concern about himself in order that he might devote every energy to the unflagging service of the sovereign Lord. Calvinism therefore bred a race of heroes.[65]

Without diluting the doctrine, predestination is, therefore, as McGrath shows in analysing Calvin's thought:

> an *ex post facto* explanation of the particularity of the human responses to grace. Calvin's predestinarianism is to be regarded as a posteriori reflection upon the data of human experience, interpreted in the light of scripture, rather than something which is deduced a priori on the basis of preconceived ideas concerning divine omnipotence. Belief in predestination is not an article of faith in its own right, but is the final outcome of scripturally informed reflection on the effects of grace upon individuals in the light of the enigmas of experience.[66]

Furthermore, one can argue, like McGrath, that there is no central dogma as such in Calvin – certainly not predestination![67] He starts the *Institutes*, rather, with the need to know God and to know ourselves.

Is there nevertheless an underlying theme to the four volumes of the *Institutes*? (Volume four deals with issues such as the church and civil government.)

I think it is safe to say that volume one makes clear the aim: 'the knowledge of God and of ourselves'.[68] Furthermore, Calvin's *Institutes* and his commentaries were not intended to be a systematic theology of the author's, but a Bible study, to show people 'what he ought especially to seek in Scripture, and to what end he ought to relate its contents'.[69] Calvin, therefore, sought to bring us back to Scripture, the great principle of the Reformation: as McGrath comments:

> Calvin is a biblical theologian. The first and foremost source of his religious ideas was the Bible. Calvin's work as a biblical commentator serves to reinforce the overall impression one gains from a close reading of the Institutes: that he regarded himself as an obedient expositor of the Bible.[70]

I emphasise this as it is something that we forget all too easily today, especially those of us (like myself) in universities or seminaries – many of you reading this book will fall into this category. Theology is about God's word, the Bible, and about the Person revealed to us in Scripture: Jesus Christ, or, as Calvin put it himself in his *Commentary on Colossians*:

Therefore, the sole means of retaining as well as restoring pure doctrine is to set Christ before our eyes, just as He is with all His blessings, that His power may be truly perceived.[71]

Protestant work ethic

Calvin has had a major influence upon us in areas more than simply theological. This is perhaps seen above all in the *social* impact of his thought.

This is something that was made famous by the work of the great early twentieth-century German writer and thinker, Max Weber, and especially in his seminal work, *The Protestant Ethic and the Spirit of Capitalism*, published in English in 1930, and his equally illustrious British contemporary, R. H. Tawney, whose book, *Religion and the Rise of Capitalism*, came out in 1926. (Together they are sometimes bracketed, for the sake of simplicity, as the 'Weber-Tawney thesis', but slightly inaccurately, I feel.)

Sadly, there is not space here to develop their arguments.[72] The Weber thesis has been widely discussed, disputed and argued over by Marxists and capitalist historians alike. The British Prime Minister, Tony Blair's sociological mentor, Anthony Giddens, has been yet another expositor of such thought.[73]

Weber came up with the theory, in a 1904 article in German, which specifically linked the rise of capitalism in the sixteenth century to Protestantism, and the thought of John Calvin in particular. One writer has said about the article:

Weber noted the statistical correlation in Germany between interest and success in capitalist ventures on the one hand and Protestant background on the other. He then went on to attribute the relationship to certain accidental psychological consequences of the notions of predestination and calling in Puritan theology, notions that were deduced with the greatest logical severity by Calvin and his followers.[74]

As we have seen, Calvin's doctrine of predestination has been misunderstood, so the description there is rather unfair. But we can probably agree with the same author when he says that the Puritans, in formulating a work ethic, 'helped to create the enormous structure of modern economic life, which came irresistibly to determine the life and values of everyone born into it'.[75]

To what extent, then, can Calvin be said to have helped found the modern capitalist age in which we live?

Alister McGrath has shown that Weber, while observationally very plausible, did not understand the *spiritual* roots of Calvin: Weber was a sociologist, not a theologian, and, as McGrath comments, this often leads to major *theological* misinterpretations: many believed in predestination long before Calvin, without any resultant rise in capitalism, and many sixteenth-century capitalists (such as the successful burghers of Amsterdam) were Arminians not Calvinists.[76]

However, it is also very true to say that Calvin legitimated ordinary work. It was as legitimate to be a roadsweep as a preacher: it all depended upon what God called you to do. There is therefore a link, but it is the doctrine of calling rather than that of predestination (which, as we have seen, comes primarily into the realm of Christian assurance rather than work), which is the clue.

As McGrath comments:

> The notion of 'calling' (*vocatio*) must be interpreted in this light: the imperative to perform good works is not necessarily linked with a specific worldly vocation... but with the need to demonstrate one's *divine* calling to oneself and the world at large.[77]

McGrath has also demonstrated that a lot of what we now call Calvinism was in fact the product of his followers after his death – of whom the Puritans are, of course, probably the best example.

So Calvin did not therefore in and of himself cause modern capitalism – in any case, the Italian (and thus Catholic) city states such as Florence, Venice and Siena had made a good start the century before. But I think that it is also fair and true to say that much of the development of specifically *modern* capitalism (from the sixteenth century onwards) does have strong Protestant links, even though the links are by no means always universal or inevitable. Furthermore, as Roland Bainton has pointed out:

> Hence one may say that Calvinism has contributed to the spirit of capitalism only if it be added that Calvinism has injected a spirit of vitality and drive into every area in which Calvinists have been disposed to enter. They have exhibited unceasing endeavour whether they were subduing a continent, overthrowing a monarchy, or managing a business, or again reforming the evils of the very order which they helped to create. Calvinists have been a strenuous breed.[78]

They have also been a tremendous credit to Calvin himself. Few men in history have had an impact as great and long-lasting as that of John Calvin. He may have dismissed himself as a timid scholar – he was deliberately, at his own request, buried in an unmarked grave, whose location is therefore unknown. But his zeal for the Gospel, often against overwhelming odds, was timeless and an example to us all. Even timid scholars can, by the grace of God, change the world!

References

1. Alister McGrath, *A Life of John Calvin* (Oxford, 1990) p. 195: the best and most accessible one volume life of Calvin subtitled, *A Study in the Shaping of Western Culture*. See also George, p. 247, for fuller quotation.

2. Britain's Scottish-raised Chancellor of the Exchequer, Gordon Brown, a son of the manse, has often been described in this way. I am sure that American readers could think of similar examples.

3. McGrath, *Life*, pp. 114-120, who points out also, for example, that Thomas Aquinas had views on Jews that we would find distasteful today. See also pp. xiii-xiv. See also George, pp. 167-169.

4. McGrath, *Life*, pp. 14-15.

5. Ibid., p. 15.

6. E. A. Dowey states so in his *Encyclopaedia Britannica* article on 'John Calvin', for example: vol. 4, 14th rev. edition (Chicago, 1972), p. 671.

7. McGrath, *Life*, pp. 21-23.

8. George, p. 171.

9. Ibid.; McGrath, *Life*, pp. 69-75: both historians deal with the issue of what exactly 'sudden' means.

10. George, p. 173; McGrath, *Life*, p. 70. I am following McGrath's translation.

11. Cameron, p. 185.

12. Dowey, p. 671; McGrath, *Life*, pp. 64-67. Dowey says Calvin played no part. McGrath is open to Calvin playing a critical role: why not decide for yourself? See also Cameron, p. 184.

13. George, p. 176.

14. Cameron, p. 185.

15. McGrath, *Life*, pp. 141-142.

16. Ibid., pp. 76-77.

17. Pages 145-174 of McGrath's book look at the teachings of

Calvin in the *Institutes* in fine detail: those wanting a digestible, but very thorough, study are recommended to go there first, since the *Institutes* themselves are heavy reading!

18. George, p. 178.

19. Ibid., p. 179.

20. McGrath, *Life*, pp. xi-xii.

21. George, p. 189; see also the chapter on Calvin's thought in Alister McGrath's more popular book, *A Cloud of Witnesses* (Leicester, 1990) pp. 90-99.

22. George, pp. 185-186.

23. Personal conversation with the author, on many occasions.

24. McGrath, *Life*, pp. 79-95 for full details.

25. George, p. 179.

26. For helpful details on the phenomenon, contrast Cameron, pp. 210-263 (on the city-states) with pp. 267-291 (on principalities and kingdoms); see also McGrath, *Life*, pp. 80-86 for a more concise and Geneva-orientated discussion of the phenomenon.

27. McGrath, *Life*, pp. 107-109.

28. George, p. 180; McGrath, *Life*, p. 95, following the translation in George, but the McGrath translation style of punctuation.

29. George, p. 180.

30. Cameron, p. 422.

31. McGrath, *Life*, p. 97. McGrath uses the word 'evangelical' which in Germany today, as 'evangelisch', is simply synonymous with Lutheran and does not now necessarily imply evangelical in the sense that many in Britain and the USA understand that term.

32. George, p. 181. See also Dowey, p. 672, who agrees.

33. Dowey, p. 672.

34. George, p. 183.

35. Ibid., p. 184.

36. Dowey, p. 672.

37. George, p. 182.

38. FFA/DW, p. 241; also see pp. 242-243.

39. Ibid., pp. 241-242.

40. Ibid., p. 242.

41. Ibid., pp. 84-85.

42. Cameron, p. 344.

43. Ibid., p. 191.

44. George, p. 182.

45. Ibid., p. 184.

46. McGrath, *Life*, p. 105; also Dowey, p. 672.

47. McGrath, *Life*, pp. 111-114.

48. Ibid., pp. 111.

49. R. M. Kingdon, 'John Calvin' in *Encyclopaedia Britannica*, Macropaedia, vol. 3, 15th edn., p. 673.

50. Hillerbrand, p. 80.

51. McGrath, *Life*, p. 113.

52. George, p. 167, who says that this is the 'common caricature'.

53. Ibid., pp. 200-201; see also 'Servetus', *Encyclopaedia Britannica*, Micropaedia, vol. ix, 15th edition, p. 75.

54. Bainton, *The Reformation of the Sixteenth Century*, p. 135.

55. Hillerbrand, pp. 70-71.

56. McGrath, *Life*, p. 115.

57. Ibid., p. 116.

58. See FFA/DW, p. 215 for a more general overview of the intolerance of those times.

59. Cameron, p. 129, and see pp. 128-132 generally; see also George, pp. 73-79 and McGrath, *Life*, p. 167.

60. George, p. 167; Timothy George seems equally puzzled.

61. For a more detailed account of these activities than is possible here, see McGrath, *Life*, pp. 174-193.

62. Cameron, p. 129; see also Hillerbrand, p. 75.

63. George, p. 232.

64. For an outstanding exposition of the relationship between the doctrine of election and evangelism, see J. I. Packer's book, *Evangelism and the Sovereignty of God* (Leicester and Downers Grove, 1961) p. 19.

65. Bainton, *The Reformation of the Sixteenth Century*, p. 117.

66. McGrath, *Life*, pp. 167-168.

67. Ibid., p. 149.

68. See George, p. 189; for a fuller and more accessible treatment see McGrath, *Life*, pp. 145-174.

69. George, p. 187.

70. McGrath, *Life*, pp. 150-151.

71. George, p. 216.

72. Two authors who discuss the connection between Calvin and

capitalism are McGrath, *Life*, pp. 21-245 and Bainton in his *The Reformation in the Sixteenth Century*, pp. 249-255; see also Cameron, pp. 301-302 and FFA/DW, pp. 277-278.

73. Anthony Giddens, *Politics and Sociology in the Thought of Max Weber* (London, 1972).

74. Arthur Mitzman, article on 'Max Weber (1864-1920)' in *Encyclopaedia Britannica, Macropaedia*, vol. 19, 15th edition, p. 715.

75. Ibid., p. 715.

76. McGrath, *Life*, pp. 237-242.

77. McGrath, *Life*, pp. 242-245.

78. *The Reformation of the Sixteenth Century*, p. 255. For more on this see McGrath, *Life*, pp. 247-261.

4

Thomas Cranmer

1489   Thomas Cranmer born

1505   goes to Cambridge University

1525   Tyndale's New Testament in English published illegally

1525   Emperor Charles V, nephew of Henry VIII's wife Catherine of Aragon, crushes the French in Italy: Rome sacked in 1527

1529   Cranmer meets Henry for the first time: suggests local theologians can decide his wish to divorce Catherine

1529   Cardinal Wolsey overthrown

1530   Cranmer begins a brief diplomatic career on Henry's behalf

1532   married to Margaret Osiander: marriage secret until 1548

1533   Cranmer officially consecrated as Archbishop of Canterbury

1533-36 Acts of Parliament breaking England's links to Rome

1536-39 Dissolution of the English monasteries

1536   Tyndale martyred. Cranmer influenced Ten Articles give new Church of England some Lutheran sympathies

1539   Six Articles, more Catholic in nature, leave Cranmer very vulnerable until Henry's death in 1547

1547   Edward VI's accession marks from political turning to Protestantism among England's ruling élite Cranmer's *Book of Homelies*

1552   Cranmer's more overtly Protestant Prayer Book

1553   Strongly reformed 42 Articles issued

1553   Edward dies and Mary I becomes Queen

1555   Cranmer's trial for heresy begins; Latimer and Ridley martyred

1556   Cranmer martyred in Oxford

1558   Mary dies; Elizabeth I, a Protestant, becomes Queen

The Reformation, when it finally came to England, came not with a Wycliffe or a Tyndale, but through the gentle scholar of quiet determination, Thomas Cranmer. Wycliffe, who was able to enjoy the political protection of John of Gaunt, Edward III's son, was fortunate to die in his bed. Tyndale, not so protected, died a martyr's death. Neither of them saw the Reformation of the Church in England, for which both of them longed.

Cranmer not only saw it arrive, he also, like Tyndale, died as a martyr – the only one of the five reformers in this book to be martyred for his beliefs.[1] (Zwingli chose to go into battle, as we saw, so his death, though violent, was not the same.)

Cranmer's violent death – burned at the stake in Oxford, just outside Balliol College, the great centre of learning where Wycliffe had been Vice-Master many years previously – sums up the reasons for Reformation in England that so distinguish it from the other four places that we are considering in this book.

The other four Reformations were arguably bottom up: they began with the grass roots desire for Reformation and, as we have seen, survived because those at the top allowed it to continue. Frederick the Wise backed something which Luther had already begun, Calvin was invited to stay in a Geneva already turning Protestant, and it was a not dissimilar case with Zwingli and Zurich. Knox, as we shall see, was effectively the spiritual adviser to a politically rebellious Protestant group, the Congregation, which seized power in Scotland.

In England, as the existence of both Wycliffe and Tyndale shows, Protestantism, or its antecedents, certainly had grass roots support. At the same time, the Cambridge academic, Eamon Duffy, in his highly influential and thoroughly researched book, *The Stripping of the Altars*,[2] has shown conclusively that English Catholicism, far from being corrupt and fading at the beginning of the sixteenth century, was if anything, alive, well and vibrant. (Indeed Duffy goes on to demonstrate that folk Catholicism, and adherence to the old ways, survived well beyond Cranmer's death and into the reign of Elizabeth I.)[3]

What then is the key factor in determining the English Reformation? What explains the present day Church of England at the beginning of the twenty-first century? A church which contains many Evangelicals, in the great Reformation-Puritan tradition, but also many so-called 'Anglo-Catholics' or 'High Church' Anglicans whose ritual practice is often not that different from (and given shifts in English Catholicism post Vatican Two, often even far more ritualistic than) that of the Roman Catholic Church?

The answer is surely the top down nature of the English Reformation, a change made initially not on spiritual grounds but on *political* ones.[4] This is how Thomas Cranmer could be promoted by one King, lauded by that King's son and martyred by the same King's elder daughter.

Thomas Cranmer was born on 2 July 1489, the son of Thomas and Agnes Cranmer. Their social status was that of lower gentry – socially well placed in the hierarchy, but without a large fortune.[5] It was therefore intended for young Thomas to enter the Church.

First of all, he had to be educated at one of the two English Universities. So in 1503 (aged fourteen, not an uncommon age to go to University in those days) he went up to Cambridge, the city in which this book is being written, and a place where Christian influence remains strong to this day. Here Cranmer flourished. Cambridge was an internationally renowned centre of learning. Erasmus, for example, spent time at Cambridge, at Queen's College.[6] In 1510 or 1511,[7] Cranmer was elected a Fellow of Jesus College, then as now the title for someone who was an official part of the scholarly community.

In those days Fellowships were often also ecclesiastical, and celibate. Cranmer, the promising and rising young scholar, suddenly threw away his planned future. He married an innkeeper's daughter named Joan. This marriage not only jeopardised his ecclesiastical future in the Church, but was also a marriage outside his social class.[8]

For a while he was able to do some teaching at Buckingham (now Magdalene) College, while his wife lived at her home, the Dolphin Inn. But as often happened in those days, his young wife died in childbirth. This was tragic for Cranmer. But it did mean that he was once again unmarried, so he was able to return to Jesus College as a Fellow once more.

Many accounts of Cranmer's life in Cambridge in the early 1520s have him as a strong Protestant sympathiser – a member of the group nicknamed 'little Germany'. This group had overt Lutheran sympathies and met to discuss theology and the latest ideas from the Continent at the White Horse Inn. William Tyndale was certainly a member of this grouping, as were other future theologians such as Robert Barnes and Thomas Bilney.[9]

Sir Geoffrey Elton, the internationally-distinguished Tudor-period historian, has Cranmer as a member of this group.[10] But recent scholarship, including a prize-winning new biography of Cranmer,[11] doubts whether Cranmer was ever a formal member of 'little Germany', and inclines rather to the view that his membership was confirmed posthumously,[12] rather than on the basis of hard *contemporary* evidence. At this distance it is difficult to tell, though it is possibly the case that people naturally presumed, in view of Cranmer's later resolutely Protestant stand, that he somehow *ought* to have been a member. But it is equally possible that for most of the 1520s Cranmer was still fairly conservative theologically and that his conversion to Protestant thought was a slower process than hitherto proposed.[13]

We now need to come on to the events which propelled Cranmer to fame – the issues at the heart of the English Reformation.

Henry VIII and his wives

People wishing to make fun of the Church of England often joke that it only came into being because King Henry VIII wanted a divorce, in order to marry the woman he loved. (In the 1990s, with Prince Charles' divorce, this issue has again become pressing in Anglican affairs.) But while this is *literally* true – Henry did want to divorce his Spanish wife, Catherine of Aragon – the issue is actually, and inevitably, far more complicated.

England in the fifteenth century had been racked by civil war, known after the event as the Wars of the Roses. It had taken Henry's father and predecessor, King Henry VII, many years to restore both military order and financial health to England. Henry VIII was the legitimate king through his mother as well as his father, and had become King in 1509 with a degree of legitimacy unknown in England for over a century.

One guarantor of the throne had been the alliance with

Spain (Castile and Aragon) – hence Henry's dynastic marriage. Now, however, the Spanish King was also Holy Roman Emperor and ruler of the present day Netherlands, Belgium and Austria, as well as of most of South America. Catherine's nephew was the Emperor Charles V, whom we saw in the chapter on Luther as the defender of Catholic Orthodoxy against the rising Protestant tide. But he also ruled over the Duchy of Milan in northern Italy and over Naples and Sicily in southern Italy, areas also coveted by the Kings of France.[14] Italy at this time was a conglomeration of numerous small states (as was Germany), some of which had foreign rulers. This semi-continuous state of war has been called the Habsburg-Valois rivalry, and much of sixteenth-century European politics became entangled in it.[15] The Pope was also the *political* ruler of a large swathe of Central Italy, known as the Papal States (or the Patrimony of St. Peter). The Papacy was thus often caught in the middle of this long-lasting dynastic rivalry, with French, Spanish, Imperial and mercenary armies marching all over Italy, Papal territory included.

During the 1520s, the Pope, Clement VII, was a member of the Medici family of Florence, the famous bankers and patrons of art. Initially Clement supported Charles V, and in 1525 Charles trounced the French forces at the Battle of Pavia. Clement now chose this unfortunate moment to switch sides, joining the pro-French league of Cognac against Charles. Charles thereupon sent a mercenary army against the Pope, and Rome was sacked in 1527,[16] the Pope being obliged to barricade himself into one of his own castles for safety. In 1528 France re-invaded Italy and the war began again.

This might seem remote from a chapter on the life of

Thomas Cranmer and the English Reformation, but on the
contrary, it is at the heart of it, and explains how it happened
in the way that it did.

In the days when it was thought that the woman
determined the sex of the child, Henry was eager to rid
himself of Catherine. Only one of their children had
survived – a girl, Mary. Catherine had previously been
married to Henry's brother Arthur, who had died young.
For dynastic-political reasons, Catherine had then been
betrothed to Henry in Arthur's place. Since the Book of
Leviticus forbade a man to marry his dead brother's widow,
Henry was only able to marry Catherine with a special Papal
dispensation from an earlier Pope. Henry now convinced
himself that God was cursing him for defying the Bible.[17]
Henry was a devout Catholic – with the help of Sir Thomas
More he had earlier written a treatise attacking Luther's
theology, for which the Pope gave Henry the title,
'Defender of the Faith'. (The Latin form of this, abbreviated
as *Fid. Def.* still appears on some coins, and remains a title
still used by the British monarchs, centuries after they
became Protestants.)

While it is easy to be cynical about Henry's spiritual
motives – he was in love with Anne Boleyn, and her sister
Mary Boleyn had been his mistress – Henry had strong
sixteenth-century dynastic reasons for wanting divorce, too.
Queens Regnant, ruling female sovereigns ruling as Queen
in their own right, were unusual in this very masculine
world. Kings had to be succeeded by *sons*, and this was
unlikely now for Henry with Catherine. The Tudor dynasty
was still new, comparatively fragile. Memories of the civil
war of the previous century were reasonably fresh. Henry
needed a male heir, and quickly.

Initially Henry went through the proper channel.[18] His own Chancellor, Cardinal Thomas Wolsey, was also the Pope's legate in England. If one Pope could give a decree dispensing with Leviticus, surely the current Pope, Clement VII, had it in his power to dispense with the dispensation, proclaim Henry's marriage to Catherine void, and allow Henry to remarry.

The politics of Italy made such a natural and obvious course completely impossible. Charles V had sacked Rome and imprisoned the Pope. No Pope in such circumstances was going to allow the Emperor's aunt to be cast off and divorced, however good the claim might be. Clement therefore stalled as much as he could, remitting the case to Rome but spinning it out as long as possible.

The divorce proceedings became known in England as the 'King's Great Matter', with Henry becoming increasingly frustrated by the slow pace of events, especially once the Pope's legate, Cardinal Campeggio, had, from Henry's point of view, begun to sabotage the formal divorce proceedings.[19]

It is at this point, in 1529, that Thomas Cranmer, the quiet Cambridge scholar, enters the story. In August 1529 Cambridge was afflicted by a sweating sickness plague. In order to avoid it, Cranmer left the city to stay away from infection, removing to the home of two of his pupils, distant relatives named Cressy, in the nearby town of Waltham in Essex.[20] The King was staying not too far away, along with two of his Councillors: Stephen Gardiner, the noted ecclesiastic and scholar, and Edward Fox. Cranmer suggested to Henry that he had the right to divorce Catherine and the right to consult *local* theologians over the matter.[21] Cranmer's idea was not unique, but it was what Henry needed to hear. It is now doubted that Cranmer, on this occasion at least, suggested an international University-wide consultation.[22] The reason for this was that as one academic joked, universities were hardly likely to go against their ruler – it was a case of *cuius regio, eius opinio.*[23]

The King ordered Cranmer to drop the other things he was doing, and to write a treatise on the vexed divorce issue. Cranmer did so, using scripture, the Church Fathers and the historic Councils of the Church as evidence to defend the validity of Henry's case (thereby, possibly proving in his use of Church Councils that his theology was more conservative at this stage than hitherto thought).[24]

In October 1529, Cardinal Wolsey, the greatest of Henry's subjects in wealth and prestige, fell from office and was only able to avoid execution by dying early of natural causes. Henry wanted to prosecute him under the medieval statute of *praemunire*,[25] which meant, in effect, that an English subject was putting allegiance to a foreign power – in Wolsey's case, the Pope – higher than the lawful allegiance to the English King. The real reason was, of course, that Wolsey had failed to obtain the divorce for which Henry yearned, though, given the exigencies of Imperial-Papal relations that we have noted, it is difficult to see how Wolsey could have succeeded.[26]

Wolsey's successor was the renowned jurist and thinker, Sir Thomas More, author of the still-read and famous book, *Utopia.*[27] More was as honest and plain living as Wolsey had been corrupt and lavish. However the idealised portrait of More in the play and film, *A Man for All Seasons*, is rather misleading;[28] as a loyal Catholic, More did not hesitate to persecute Protestants, and he condemned them to the same violent end which he was later to meet himself.

Further, the film is also rather harsh in its portrayal of the one key survivor from Wolsey's regime, Thomas Cromwell, who now moved into a position of considerable power as a royal official, becoming Principal Secretary in 1534.[29] Cromwell was a convinced Protestant for whom the impending break with Rome created spiritual as well as political opportunities. Historians debate whether Cromwell was the great innovator and moderniser portrayed by G. R. Elton in the 1950s, but whether or not there was a Tudor revolution in government,[30] Cromwell was surely a promoter of the Reformation in England and someone who would be a key collaborator for Cranmer in the crucial years ahead.[31]

Henry's instinct was to put pressure on the Church in the hope that they in turn would put pressure on Rome. So in December 1530, Henry's Attorney General pressed charges against the Church, including their need to acknowledge him as the 'protector and only supreme head of the English Church and Clergy'.[32] The Convocation of the Church met and duly paid an enormous fine to Henry, acknowledging his title with the careful caveat 'so far as the law of Christ allows'.[33] However Henry was no nearer getting a divorce, and the stalemate continued.

Henry's gratitude to Cranmer for writing his treatise was considerable. Cranmer now rose from the seclusion of Cambridge on to the national, and then international, stage. He made the acquaintance of the now influential Boleyn family.[34] He was made a Chaplain to the king, Rector of Bredon in Worcestershire[35], then later on in 1531, Archdeacon of Taunton.[36] In 1530, Cranmer and Anne Boleyn's father, the Earl of Wiltshire, were sent as English emissaries to Rome itself, to plead Henry's case before the Papal authorities. Within one year Cranmer had been transformed from an obscure scholar into a major player.

Although Cranmer was given the title 'Grand Penitentiary of England'[37] by the Pope, it was not surprising that no progress was made in Rome over the divorce issue. So in 1532 Cranmer was sent to Nuremburg, where the German Princes would be meeting. In theory he was to see Emperor Charles V – with whom some effective political power over the Pope still lay – but in practice to see the Lutheran Princes who would be there, to see what kind of help could be obtained.

Here Cranmer took another very human, quite natural, yet career-foolish step: he fell in love with Margaret,[38] the niece of Andreas Osiander, a leading Lutheran.[39] Clerical marriage was firmly forbidden in England – indeed not until 1548, with the thoroughly Protestant King Edward VI on the throne, was Cranmer able to acknowledge openly that he was a happily married man. Still, his action shows a strong moral tone to Cranmer – he married her rather than making her his mistress. Concubinage was not uncommon among pre-Reformation clergy. He also showed what Elton has described as a lack of ambition,[40] or, what I would prefer to call a wonderful unworldliness – ambitious men in the Church would never dream of getting married, as to do so would still be a firm block on the road to promotion.

When Henry realised that diplomacy was getting nowhere, he began to turn to more drastic financial pressure. In 1532, therefore, he began proceedings in Parliament whereby the English dues owed to Rome would be cut off. Parliament passed the Conditional Restraint on Annates, which forbade the payment of revenue to Rome.[41] The same year saw the Submission of the Clergy, granted in response to a request by the House of Commons,[42] which protested vigorously against what they held to be the manifold abuses of the Church heaped upon the English people. Henry joined in the attack, in which he stated that the clergy were only half-subjects, since they had also sworn allegiance to the Pope. The Submission was too much for Sir Thomas More, who promptly resigned the Chancellorship, pleading ill health. The Archbishop of Canterbury, Warham, agreed to the Submission, but died in August 1532, not long after making it, creating a critical vacancy at a key moment in the debate.

Archbishop of Canterbury

But rather than give the archbishopric to the favourite choice, Stephen Gardiner,[43] Henry conferred it instead on Cranmer,[44] who was thereby propelled into the leading spiritual post in the English church's hierarchy. Cranmer was formally consecrated as Archbishop, and thus Primate of the Church of England, the senior ecclesiastic, in March 1533.[45]

Thomas Cromwell was doing all possible to accelerate the divorce proceedings on Henry's behalf. He now had as Archbishop of Canterbury someone with whom he could collaborate on the King's Great Matter.

Cranmer had provided the King with *spiritual* justification; Cromwell provided the *political* rationale for the break. To him, England was an Empire, owing allegiance to no one.[46] This meant that England had the political freedom to do what she liked, without anyone's permission.

This was to make a critical difference to the English

Reformation – one can describe it as a political revolution with spiritual results. As we shall see, a lot of what Cranmer could and could not do depended in very large measure on the degree of political support available.

This political reasoning was used in the Act in Restraint of Appeals in 1533.[47] In essence it meant that all appeals regarding spiritual jurisdiction were to be heard within England – the Archbishop of Canterbury, not the Pope, would determine all such issues. This in turn meant that the new Archbishop, Cranmer, had the sole right to determine the issue of the divorce. Consequently, in May 1533, Cranmer convened a Court in Dunstable which proclaimed that Henry's marriage to Catherine had been void from the beginning, and that the king was now free to marry Anne Boleyn.[48] Henry and Anne could now marry, which was just as well, since Anne was already pregnant with Henry's child.[49] Cromwell was now able to produce a series of statutes to effect a new Government for the Church of England – one that would be under local political control rather than that of the distant Pope.

Historians differ as to the extent to which this reflected the religious sentiments of ordinary English people. The traditional view, put forward by the distinguished Tudor specialist, A. G. Dickens, is that England was becoming increasingly Protestant in faith as well as in legal name.[50] While it might be spiritually pleasant for pro-Reformation sympathisers to think of this being the case,[51] nonetheless Eamon Duffy's groundbreaking work does seem to point to the fact that Dickens and others are mistaken in terms of historical fact, and that traditional English belief was, far from being rotten and on the decline, in fact very much alive.[52]

This makes the political backing for change all the more

important, especially the activities of Cromwell from 1525 up until 1539, when a theologically conservative reaction set in.[53] If indeed the bulk of the English population remained theologically conservative, as Duffy's work suggests, one could argue that what created the English Reformation was a brilliant seizure of opportunity by Protestants in key positions, such as Cranmer and Cromwell, caused by the desire of an innately theologically conservative King for a male heir and the political stability that such dynastic continuity would bring.[54]

As we shall see from the end of this chapter, it was a close-run thing. Had Mary had longer on the throne, or had she been able to locate a successful Catholic successor, then it is conceivable that the Reformation might not have lasted.[55] As it did survive, we tend to think that its survival was inevitable – but I think that it is legitimate to argue that we can really only say this with hindsight. When we look, therefore, at all that Cranmer achieved in the twenty years 1533-1553, we must always remember the politically and spiritually very precarious background against which he did what he did.

While Cranmer was settling in to office, Cromwell busied himself with the legal technicalities of the new Church. The key was the royal ecclesiastical supremacy, and an Act of Supremacy, recognising Henry as Supreme Head of the Church in England, was duly passed in 1534.[56] (The Pope had excommunicated Henry the previous year.) It became treasonable to deny Henry's title, or the lawfulness of his marriage to Anne Boleyn. (It was More's refusal to accept these legal/political changes which led to his execution in 1535.) All appeals and sending money to Rome were now expressly forbidden.

Cranmer, supported by Cromwell, set out on some initial spiritual reforms. (Cromwell was appointed the King's Vicegerent in spirituals, i.e. spiritual affairs of the Church.)

The new Ten Articles of 1536 set out the beliefs of the Church of England.[57] Influenced strongly by Melanchthon, they put forward a Lutheran view of justification by faith, and introduced mild liturgical reforms that bore the stamp of suggestions made years earlier by Erasmus. In particular, the Lutheran view of justification by faith became the new official doctrine. Official *Injunctions* were issued in 1536 and 1538 to enforce the Articles.[58]

Perhaps most important of all in the long term, clergy were required to preach from the Bible. Here there was a major and drastic change: no longer was the Bible in English forbidden.[59] It was, by contrast, positively encouraged, with Miles Coverdale's English Bible becoming the approved translation in 1535[60] and the Great Bible coming out in 1539, a translation in which Cranmer played a major role as to its appearance.[61] As in Luther's Germany, people were being actively urged to read God's Word in their own language.

Last of all, the *Bishop's Book* was issued, something that Euan Cameron has aptly described as 'a bewilderingly ambiguous amalgam of reformed ideas about the Church and modest recommendations on worship'[62], perhaps because it was produced by an endless series of committees and discussions.[63] The possible reason for this slightly ambiguous state of affairs has been stated as follows: 'to propound theological notions in Henry's England after the break with Rome was rather like walking a tightrope. The argument had to be both antipapal and pro-Catholic, a combination of ingredients that required an exquisite measure of theological balance or versatility.'[64]

Cranmer was able to walk such a tightrope – it is why, despite the many attempts of his enemies, he was able to survive under Henry until 1547. For while Henry was firm about his royal ecclesiastical supremacy, the rest of him remained, arguably, firmly Catholic in doctrine.

One of Henry's measures unwittingly helped the long-term Protestant cause. This was the dissolution of the monasteries: the smaller monasteries in 1536 and the larger ones in 1539.[65] In terms of cultural destruction, the effect was devastating, as countless objects and books of great beauty were ruthlessly destroyed. The official reason was the sin of the monks, but the fact that the first dissolution was done on the basis of the wealth of the monasteries concerned makes this a slightly dubious pretext. Since monasteries were often the sources of education and hospital care, as well as being spiritual centres of contemplation, the effect on ordinary people, who relied on the monasteries for teaching and medical care, was as cataclysmic as for the monks and nuns being expelled. The monasteries, being major landowners as well, were also major local employers in their locations, and this too meant that their dissolution caused extensive upheaval.

The takeover of the monasteries initially meant a vast augmentation of royal power: at a time when agriculture was a lynchpin of economic prosperity, some of the prime real estate of England suddenly found its way to the hands of the king. However, Henry's wars, especially between 1542-1546, caused him to sell an enormous part of the new royal estate. Land was sold; it would not have been economic simply to give it as gifts to court favourites. Overnight England had a major, comparatively new

landowning class, men with vast landed estates made up
of former monastic lands. If you go to Woburn Abbey, for
example, the Russell family, from whom the Dukes of
Bedford and the twentieth-century philosopher Bertrand
Russell are descended, you can actually see where the
original monastic cloisters, now part of the great Tudor
manor house, once stood.

For such beneficiaries, Catholic restoration could mean
the loss of their newly bought estates and newly acquired
great wealth. Such powerful members of the political elite
thereby had a very literal vested interest in the maintenance
of Protestantism in England: the land and newly built
houses in which they lived.

Cranmer himself, however, had very little indeed to do
with this momentous event.[66] The initiative lay with
Thomas Cromwell. Cranmer's energies were elsewhere,
such as in discussions over the *Bishop's Book* with Henry
VIII,[67] whose strong amateur interest in theology
remained.[68] In the discussion, one can see both Henry's
innate theological conservatism and the way in which
Cranmer was moving in an ever more Reformed direction.
As Cranmer's biographer, MacCulloch, puts it, 'When
reading Cranmer's comments on the doctrinal formulations
of the Church of England, King Henry could not have hoped
to hear a clearer exposition of the once-for-all character of
justification by faith, controlled by the logic of
predestination, than he did in Cranmer's annotations.'[69]

Rebellions broke out against the newly imposed church
settlement, the most notable of these being the Pilgrimage
of Grace in 1536.[70] Such revolts were all suppressed, but
they caused much worry to the theological conservatives
at Court, notably the great magnate the Duke of Norfolk[71]

and Cranmer's ecclesiastical rival, Stephen Gardiner, the Bishop of Winchester.

Cranmer's remarkable capacity for survival amidst all the sometimes – violent ups and downs of Tudor politics can be seen in the events leading to the fall of Anne Boleyn.[72] As we saw, Cranmer was close to the Boleyn family – their patronage had certainly done no harm. But Anne had failed to produce the longed-for male heir. (The fact that her child by Henry, Elizabeth, was to reign from 1558 to1603 as one of England's most illustrious and outstanding monarchs is one of the greatest ironies of British history – one that would have astounded the traditionalist and chauvinist Henry.) Cranmer was able to procure a divorce for Henry, on the basis of supposed adultery by Anne, who was later executed – how genuinely guilty Anne was is at this remove rather difficult to tell. Anne died, but Cranmer survived. Henry's next wife, Jane Seymour, produced the longed-for male heir, Edward, but tragically died in childbirth, leaving Henry a widower.

With Henry's own theology being innately conservative, Norfolk and Gardiner were able to have the *Six Articles* introduced and enforced in 1539.[73] The six points reinforced were the traditional doctrines of transubstantiation, Communion in two 'species', celibacy, clerical chastity and auricular confession, and were seen by convinced Protestants as 'whip[s] with six strings'.[74]

Meanwhile Cromwell unwittingly played into their hands. Eager to form alliances with Lutheran powers in Germany, he married Henry to Anne of Cleves,[75] an indisputably Protestant princess. Henry, unfortunately, disliked her on sight, likening her to a horse from Flanders! Cromwell's fall was swift and in 1540 he was executed on spurious charges of treason. The conservative court faction of Norfolk and Gardiner was triumphant.

Cranmer now worked in a low-key manner, producing a new litany in 1543 and a primer in 1544, all the while managing to survive.[76] Cranmer's survival through these dark days has been the cause of much discussion. Perhaps, as we shall see, it was his otherworldliness. But was it something else? Perhaps it was his patience – a realisation that things would have to come slowly, rather than rapidly, that it was better to get there eventually rather than not at all? This is certainly what Bucer seemed to think, in defending Cranmer against those who thought that the perfect church should be easy to accomplish.[77] Cranmer, therefore, might have been a tortoise rather than a hare – but then it was the tortoise that won the race in the fable, not the hare.

The Act of Six Articles and the death of Cromwell left Cranmer rather exposed. His enemies plotted on several occasions to have him removed on the grounds of heresy – a guilty conviction would have proved literally fatal. However, Cranmer had a protector in the King himself, despite Henry's own innate conservatism. It seems that Henry liked Cranmer personally, which certainly helped. More important – and G. R. Elton is surely right[78]– in an age of plots, counterplots, intrigue, subterfuge and Court faction fighting, Henry found in Cranmer a rare man: someone he could actually trust. He was not devious, self-promoting or avaricious – he was no Cardinal Wolsey with a private agenda of his own matched by a desire to accumulate a vast personal fortune. The downside of this, as Elton also observes, is that Cranmer was given little *political* influence. This probably had the effect of keeping

Cranmer out of the vicious factional atmosphere, which grew as Henry became increasingly incapacitated. While it meant that Cranmer had less power than had traditionally been given to senior ecclesiastics, it did, though, have the benefit of keeping him alive in a political environment in which to lose politically sometimes meant to lose your life as well.

Reign of Edward VI

In 1547 Henry died and his sickly young son Edward came to the throne as Edward VI. The new King was a deeply convinced Protestant.[79] Henry had originally envisaged a ruling group to rule until Edward came of age. But recent scholarship has suggested that a group of active Protestants in the Privy Chamber (or Private Office in modern language) managed to manipulate the will to enable Edward's maternal uncle, Edward Seymour, to seize power as Lord Protector, becoming also Duke of Somerset in the process.[80]

Somerset was more of a soldier than a politician, and his rule was not a great success, ending in a series of popular uprisings.[81] But it did create an environment in which Cranmer and other of the more overtly Protestant Bishops were able to bring in some further reforms, without the *Six Articles* to restrain them any more.[82] Cranmer was cautious.[83] He did not want people to think that Protestantism was being rushed in too quickly by a court faction taking advantage of a royal minority. However, he certainly took advantage of his new-found theological freedom.

Consequently, in 1547, Cranmer was able to bring in a new *Book of Homilies*,[84] designed to encourage preaching as an integral part of Christian worship, and also to strengthen the Reformation doctrine of 'salvation as God's free gift of grace by faith'.[85] Cranmer had written forerunners of the homilies during Henry VIII's reign,[86] but it was only now, under the new regime of the young 'Josiah', as Edward VI was known,[87] that he could really get going.

In 1549 Somerset was overthrown by the far more ruthless fellow soldier and courtier John Dudley, Earl of Warwick, who became Duke of Northumberland and ruler of England for the remainder of Edward's reign. While Northumberland's own faith remains ambiguous, he was, in practice, fully behind the project to make England a thorough-going Protestant country. This meant that for Reformers such as Cranmer, the state was now fully behind ecclesiastical reform, rather than a brake to it as had been the case for the previous twenty years. Now the English Reformation really could be a *spiritual* one as well as something that had been primarily political rather than theological in motivation.

A new Prayer Book came into effect in 1549,[88] dismissed by some of Cranmer's more Evangelical critics as being too cautious,[89] but possibly, as Bucer felt, because Cranmer was being clever in getting a stop-gap measure while working on something more substantial and overtly Protestant.[90] This Prayer Book was followed in 1552 by another one which was still more overtly Protestant.[91] The latter was influenced by Martin Bucer, now living in England as a Professor at Cambridge University. Several leading Continental Protestants came to England:[92] Peter Martyr was a Professor at Oxford, for example, and Jan Laski,[93] a Polish exile, better known as John à Lasco, was a great influence on Cranmer's theological thinking,[94] although less so as time went on.[95]

The key theological dogma of the Eucharist, on which Cranmer had been pondering as early as Henry VIII's reign, was decidedly Reformed in flavour, influenced more by the thinkers of Strasbourg, such as Bucer,[96] rather than Luther, who, as we have seen, disagreed strongly with Zwingli and the Swiss Reformers on the subject.

Cranmer also wanted to include as much Protestant continental thought as he could, so that the English version of the Evangelical faith would have the best of the new thinking from the Lutherans through to the Swiss.[97] This was, of course, a hard task, with Cranmer aiming to do the best he could.

In 1553 Cranmer produced his *42 Articles* of official doctrinal belief for the Church of England.[98] Not only was this strongly Reformed in tone, it was also made a benchmark for all appointments. Schoolmasters and University teachers as well as Anglican clergy had to assent to its statements in order to gain a position.[99]

Just as Reformed thinking reached its English apogee, tragedy struck. The fatal problem for a politically introduced church, one founded on monarchical power, was that it depended on royal support for its existence. Edward VI, now increasingly frail, died in 1553.[100]

Mary becomes Queen

Northumberland, who had married his son, Lord Guildford Dudley, to Edward's distant cousin, Lady Jane Grey (a descendant of Henry VII through Henry's daughter Mary), attempted a *coup d'etat*. Although Lady Jane's genealogical claim was remote, she was an unquestioned, resolute

Protestant. Northumberland therefore skipped over the more obvious Protestant choice, Elizabeth (Henry VIII's daughter by Anne Boleyn), to place Lady Jane on the throne. She was Queen for only nine days, replaced by her cousin Mary Tudor (Henry VIII's daughter by Catherine of Aragon), who, as Edward VI's oldest half-sister, had a far greater dynastic claim.[101] In the one successful rebellion of the Tudor period, Mary overthrew Jane to become Queen.

England now had a resolutely Catholic sovereign, someone determined to restore the country to its original pre-Reformation faith.[102] It is perhaps a vindication of Eamon Duffy's *Stripping of the Altars* thesis that grass roots Catholicism, or certainly Catholic sentiment, was still strong enough to make Mary's spiritual counter-revolution possible.[103]

Cranmer was thus in dire peril, as the author of the highly overt Protestant reforms under Edward. Many leading Protestants fled to the continent, but Cranmer was brave enough to stay put.[104]

Not surprisingly, he was soon arrested though under the pretext of support for Lady Jane Grey, rather than for heresy. A heresy law against Protestantism was introduced in 1555, and Cranmer was duly condemned on 14 February 1556 after a long trial which began in October 1555.[105]

In this situation Cranmer shows his very human side. While one can imagine the other four subjects of this book boldly going defiant to the stake, Cranmer, the only actual martyr of the five, initially recanted his Protestant beliefs.[106] He was, as has been said of him, a 'very human man', essentially a gentle scholar, not a zealot.[107] It is easy for those of us who live in the comfort of the West to condemn what looks like cowardice; but, faced with a gruesome, painful death, how brave would we *really* be?

Furthermore, in October 1555, he had been forced to watch the gruesome burning at the stake in Oxford of fellow Protestants Latimer and Ridley. Latimer's famous last words, 'Be of good comfort, Master Ridley, and play the man. We shall this day light such a candle, by God's grace, in England, as I trust shall never be put out', were to echo around England and the Continent.[108]

Then, just before he was about to die, Cranmer's heroism returned.[109] To the consternation of his accusers, he denounced his recantation and faced death as an unrepentant Protestant.[110] He was martyred in Oxford on 21 March 1556, thrusting the hand with which he had signed the recantation into the flames.

After Mary's death in 1558, England became a Protestant country again, with the accession of Elizabeth I. Elizabeth, while Protestant, was innately more cautious, and the Church of England was not as overtly Reformed in emphasis as it was in its Edwardian heyday.[111] Eventually the Puritans were to split away, and in 1662 many were formally expelled.[112]

Cranmer's political legacy was therefore mixed. Today the Church of England has a mix of thoroughly Reformed and Evangelical, alongside Anglo-Catholics and theological liberals. His liturgical legacy, however, remains, its magnificent literary style still with us. England remains a Protestant country, Cranmer's theological legacy as powerful as it has ever been.

References

1. Diarmaid MacCulloch, *Thomas Cranmer* (London and New Haven) 1996, pp. 603-605. The spot of Cranmer's death is marked with a metal cross on the street, sadly now usually covered by a parked car – the memorial to the Martyrs, who included Latimer and Ridley, is around the corner in St. Giles.

2. (London and New Haven, 1992) *passim*. Duffy is a Catholic, but has attracted many Evangelical pupils over the years.

3. Ibid., pp. 565-593.

4. Timothy George, p. 98, points out that Calvin, Luther, Zwingli and Cranmer were all *magisterial Reformers*, i.e., those who carried out the Reformation with the full collaboration of secular princes. As we will see in my chapter on Knox, I will argue that Protestantism essentially came to power in Scotland through a political *coup* – in that sense, therefore, all five of the Reformers in this book can effectively come into the *magisterial* category.

5. For a detailed look at Cranmer's social background and its implications, see MacCulloch, pp. 7-15.

6. Ibid., p. 21; see also G. R. Elton, ed., 'Thomas Cranmer' in *The Encyclopaedia Britannica*, Macropaedia, vol. 5, 15th rev. edn. (Chicago, 1975) p. 236. For the dates quoted here, see also *Erasmus and Cambridge*, ed. with notes by H. C. Porter; translator D. F. S. Thomson (Toronto, 1963).

7. Elton, 'Thomas Cranmer', p. 236; MacCulloch, pp. 20-21; Hillerbrand, pp. 112-113 feels that initially the young band of scholars meeting for theological discussion at The White Horse Inn in Cambridge was probably more excited by Erasmus than by Luther.

8. Elton, p. 236; see also MacCulloch, pp. 21-22.

9. Cameron, p. 281; Hillerbrand, pp. 112-113.

10. In Elton, 'Thomas Cranmer', p. 236; so too does Cameron, p.281.

11. MacCulloch, p. 25.

12. Foxe's famous sixteenth-century *Book of Martyrs*. See MacCulloch, p. 25 for the flaws.

13. MacCulloch, pp. 24-33.

14. For a treatment of how Charles V tried to juggle so much at the same time, see the sympathetic portrayal by a twentieth-century member of that family, Otto von Habsburg, *Charles V*; and also the

references to Charles in the Luther chapter of this book and Hillerbrand, pp. 109-110.

15. For a succinct account of this often complex dynastic strife, see F. C. Spooner, 'The Habsburg-Valois Struggle', in G. R. Elton, ed., *The New Cambridge Modern History*, vol. 2 (Cambridge, 1958) pp. 334-358.

16. Hillerbrand, p. 183 (and pp. 182-183 for a discussion of the wider complications for the Papacy); Spooner, pp. 344-345; Cameron, p. 281 for the specifically English implications.

17. Hillerbrand, pp. 114-116.

18. Ibid., pp. 115-116.

19. MacCulloch, p. 44, who suggests that Campeggio's actions finally sundered Henry's faith in the Papacy.

20. MacCulloch, p. 45.

21. Ibid., pp. 45-46.

22. Elton, 'Thomas Cranmer', pp. 236-237.

23. MacCulloch, p. 45.

24. Ibid., pp. 29-30 and p. 47, where MacCulloch points out that ascribing exact authorship to Cranmer for some articles is problematic; see another view in Hillerbrand, p. 116, who suggests that Cranmer based his view on scripture rather than on church councils.

25. Hillerbrand, p. 116.

26. Cameron, p. 281.

27. See G. R. Elton's piece, 'Constitutional Development and Political Thought in Western Europe' in *New Cambridge Modern History*, op. cit., pp. 459-460 for a discussion of the impact of this remarkable book.

28. See, for example, Cameron, pp. 231 and 282; for a more sympathetic portrait of More, see Peter Ackroyd's *Life of Thomas More* (London, 1998).

29. See Hillerbrand, p. 118 for a summary view.

30. For a far more detailed view, see G. R. Elton's famous work, *England under the Tudors* (Cambridge, 1953) which portrays Cromwell as a revolutionary administrative genius. Elton summarises his own view in 'Constitutional Developments', pp. 447-448. For a more up-to-date view see the provocative historian David Starkey's book, *The Reign of Henry VIII* (London, 1991) pp. 103-123 and p.169 (on Starkey's revisionism). See also Dickens, *The English Reformation*, pp. 112-113.

31. Cameron, p. 283, shows that Cromwell was someone of firmly Lutheran views; MacCulloch, p. 173, is more cynical about what Cromwell believed precisely and when, but concedes that Lutheranism influenced his changing religious opinions.

32. Hillerbrand, p. 117; Cameron, p. 282.

33. Ibid.

34. MacCulloch, p. 47.

35. Ibid., p. 49.

36. Ibid., pp. 67-68, in succession to his Cambridge contemporary, future rival and eventual nemesis, Stephen Gardiner. MacCulloch suggests that this means that Gardiner and Cranmer were not theologically so far apart at this stage, i.e., that Cranmer was still relatively conservative in thought.

37. Or Penitentiary-General; see MacCulloch, pp. 48-49.

38. Elton, 'Thomas Cranmer', p. 237, and MacCulloch, pp. 69-76 for a fuller discussion of the marriage.

39. MacCulloch, pp. 70-71 and 72.

40. Elton, 'Thomas Cranmer', p. 238.

41. Hillerbrand, p. 117.

42. Ibid., pp. 117-118.

43. Elton, 'The Reformation in England', *New Cambridge Modern History*, p. 234.

44. MacCulloch, pp. 83-84; Cameron, p. 282.

45. MacCulloch, p. 88.

46. Hillerbrand, p. 118; Elton, 'The Reformation', op. cit., p. 234; Dickens, pp. 117-118.

47. Hillerbrand, p. 118; MacCulloch, pp. 88-91.

48. MacCulloch, pp. 92-94.

49. Ibid., pp. 94-98; Elizabeth was born three months after her parents' marriage.

50. Dickens, pp. vi and 83-108.

51. For example, many Evangelical readers will be much in sympathy with Dickens' views, as, for instance, op. cit., pp. 135-138, where Dickens discusses the history of the Great Bible.

52. Duffy, pp. 5-6 for a general statement of Duffy's views on the strength of traditional religious sentiment and pp. 479 ff. for a more specific rebuttal of the theories of Dickens and others that traditional English religion was both rotten and on the way out; see by contrast

Dickens' own view in Dickens, p. 137 and pp. 326-327.

53. Dickens, pp. 110 and 10-141, as well as 179: here I have no reason to disagree with Dickens' analysis.

54. My own view, based upon a synthesis of the differing views.

55. See, for example, Duffy, pp. 562-563; see by contrast, Hillerbrand, p. 136 and Cameron, p. 285; see also MacCulloch, p. 620 and Elton, 'The Reformation', p. 249.

56. Hillerbrand, p. 120.

57. Cameron, p. 282; Duffy, pp. 392-394 (especially on the ambiguity on Purgatory's existence); MacCulloch, pp. 161-162 and 164-166, who points out that the more conservative faction were able to get their way on some of the articles, notably Article 3 on penance.

58. Hillerbrand, p. 124; Cameron, p. 283; MacCulloch, p. 166.

59. MacCulloch, p. 166 and p. 196 for Cromwell's support.

60. Ibid., p. 166; plus Hillerbrand, pp. 124-125; see also Dickens, pp. 134-138.

61. MacCulloch, pp. 196-197 and 238-240: MacCulloch shows how very excited Cranmer was about the project.

62. Cameron, p. 283.

63. For details, see MacCulloch, pp. 185-197; see also Hillerbrand, p. 120.

64. Hillerbrand, p. 119.

65. Ibid., pp. 122-123.

66. MacCulloch, p. 135.

67. Ibid., pp. 205-207.

68. Ibid., pp. 208-209.

69. Ibid., p. 212.

70. Hillerbrand, pp. 123-124; MacCulloch, pp. 169-172, for Cranmer's low profile during the uprising.

71. Dickens, pp. 172-173.

72. MacCulloch, pp. 154-159. MacCulloch criticises Cranmer for being craven in not standing up more for the Boleyns, but then, had he done so, he might have been executed too, in those violent times. See also Starkey, pp 108-115.

73. Cameron, p. 283; MacCulloch, pp. 237-258.

74. Hillerbrand, p. 125.

75. See Starkey, pp. 124-145 for an account of all the court intrigue.

76. Cameron, p. 283.

77. For the debate, and Bucer's response to Cranmer about one of Cranmer's continental critics, see MacCulloch, pp. 235-236.

78. Elton, 'Thomas Cranmer', p. 237.

79. Hillerbrand, p. 128; Duffy, p. 448.

80. For a detailed account of the intrigues, which were greatly to help the Protestant cause, see Starkey, pp. 147-167.

81. Cameron, p. 284.

82. Hillerbrand, pp. 128-129.

83. Duffy, p. 448.

84. Elton, 'Thomas Cranmer', p. 237; Duffy, pp. 448-449.

85. MacCulloch, p. 373.

86. Ibid., p. 372.

87. Ibid., p. 349 and Duffy, p. 448.

88. See Hillerbrand, p. 129, and Duffy, pp. 464-469 for its day to day influence.

89. Cameron, p. 284.

90. MacCulloch, pp. 410-411.

91. Hillerbrand, pp. 130-131; Duffy, pp. 472-477.

92. Cameron, p. 284.

93. Elton, 'Thomas Cranmer', pp. 237-238.

94. MacCulloch, p. 394.

95. Ibid., pp. 478-479.

96. See MacCulloch, pp. 381-385, and Cameron, p. 284 for Bucer's influence on the 1552 Prayer Book.

97. Ibid., pp. 390-392; Hillerbrand, p. 129.

98. Cameron, p. 284; MacCulloch, p. 500 *passim* up to p. 538.

99. Elton, 'Thomas Cranmer', 238.

100. Elton, 'Reformation', p. 246.

101. Hillerbrand, p. 131; MacCulloch, p. 538 and pp. 540-544 for Cranmer's role as a member of the Council which proclaimed Jane as Queen.

102. Hillerbrand, pp. 132-133; Elton, 'The Reformation', pp. 246-247.

103. Duffy's section on Queen Mary, pp. 524-564 *passim*.

104. MacCulloch, pp. 548-549, shows how brave Cranmer was.

105. Ibid., pp. 572-580 for the full details of Cranmer's trial.

106. Hillerbrand, pp. 135-136.

107. Elton, 'Thomas Cranmer', p. 238; Hillerbrand, p. 136 says

that Matthew Parker, Queen Elizabeth I's Archbishop of Canterbury, wrote of Cranmer, 'we are all human beings'.

108. MacCulloch, p. 582.

109. Hillerbrand, p. 136; MacCulloch, pp. 601 and 603.

110. MacCulloch, pp. 603-605.

111. Ibid., pp. 620-622; Hillerbrand, pp. 137-146; Cameron, p. 286 and pp. 381-385.

112. One of the most eminent to be expelled was the Puritan Richard Baxter, whose works are still read and studied today: see the article on 'Richard Baxter' in F. L. Cross, ed., *The Oxford Dictionary of the Christian Church* (Oxford and New York, 1957).

5

John Knox

1514 John Knox born

1540 Knox ordained a priest

1543-47 Knox becomes more Protestant in sympathy

1547 becomes involved in a Protestant rebellion based
      in St Andrews. This fails and Knox spends eight-
      teen months as a French galley slave

1551 appointed to a position in Newcastle (England);
      active in the Edwardian Reformation

1553 has to flee again on Mary's accession; spends exile
      in Geneva and Frankfurt

1556 Knox's *Letter of Wholesome Counsel*

1558 His first *Blast of the Trumpet*

1559 Knox able to return to Scotland; pro-Reformation
      forces seize power

1561 Mary Queen of Scots's return blights Knox's hopes

1567 Mary flees but situation continues unstable

1571 Knox himself has to flee Edinburgh as civil strife
      continues

1572 Knox dies

John Knox, the spiritual leader of the Scottish Reformation, was born around 1514 in the town of Haddington, near Edinburgh.[1] This date, puts him, with Calvin, in the second generation of Reformation leaders.

We tend to think of Scotland as being somehow a more spiritually-minded place than England, a country where theological thinking and influence is more pervasive than in her more powerful neighbour to the south, a feeling which pervades even the twentieth century. How likely is it that an English equivalent to that great Scottish missionary and athletic hero, Eric Liddell, in *Chariots of Fire*, would have had the same degree of credibility? The Scots appear to take their faith more seriously, and heavily Christianised areas of Scotland, such as the Highlands and Islands, have no real English equivalent. In turn, Scottish spirituality has had a major impact on areas of Scottish emigration, such as Northern Ireland and the USA.

All this can be deemed to be part of the spiritual legacy of John Knox. Yet what is interesting is that Scottish Protestantism did not prevail until a whole generation after its English counterpart, and that, far from being a mass movement, the Reformation can in a real sense be said to have originated in a political *coup d'etat*[2] in 1560, when Knox himself was over forty-five. So while Knox's great hero, Calvin, came to an already Protestant Geneva, Protestantism's rise in Scotland was a long process, often perilous, one in which its leaders had to struggle long to see their faith prevail.

In other words, Knox's career demonstrates that the prevalence of the Reformation over much of Europe was as much a *political* process as a *spiritual* one, where the consent of the secular ruler made a significant difference as to whether or not the Reformation succeeded.

As with Calvin, very little is known about Knox's early life.[3] He came from a family of farmers, with a father named William. The theory is that he studied theology for the priesthood[4] – in a church that was still thoroughly Catholic and unreformed. His teacher at St. Andrew's University was the distinguished scholar, John Major (sic!). Knox did not remain to take his M.A. degree, but, as the writer James McEwen has pointed out, his mental training was recognised throughout Europe as being quintessentially Scottish in influence.[5]

Knox was certainly an ordained priest by 1540. He must have been in good standing with the ecclesiastical hierarchy, because by 1543 he held the minor post of apostolic notary. However, at some as yet fully undetermined point, by 1545, Knox was a tutor in East Lothian in the households of two gentry (or minor/untitled aristocratic) families, both of which were known for their Protestant sympathies. In particular, they protected the notable Scottish Protestant preacher of the time, George Wishart.[6] Wishart began a major preaching tour in the Lothians area of southern Scotland in December 1545. One thing we do know almost for certain is that this tour had a considerable influence upon Knox, and that his conversion to Reformed thinking can probably be dated to around this time. However, in March 1546, Wishart was arrested and burned at the stake as a heretic on the orders of Cardinal David Beaton, the Bishop of St. Andrews, who was also one of the key political figures of Scotland at this time.

The often violent nature of sixteenth-century life can be seen in the fact that three months later Beaton was himself murdered by Protestant leaders, who had been outraged by Wishart's death. Knox was linked in the eyes of the authorities to the Protestant laymen who had carried out the deed. He wanted to flee to Germany after Beaton's murder, knowing that he would be much safer there, in Protestant territory. However his aristocratic protectors obliged him to stay with them in St. Andrew's, where they needed his spiritual counsel. The Protestant forces now controlled the castle in the town, and this is where Knox found himself there in April 1547. As McEwen has written, Knox now became, unwittingly, the main Protestant, pro-Reformation preacher in Scotland.[7]

Not surprisingly, Knox realised fully that this placed him in a politically very precarious, high profile, position.[8] It was not long since Wishart's martyrdom, and if the defenders of St. Andrews lost to the authorities, there was a good chance that he would soon meet a similarly violent end. Knox therefore tearfully resisted the call to public ministry, protesting that he was a quiet scholar. But in the end he gave in and began what was to go on to become a famous Reformed preaching ministry. So powerful and persuasive was his preaching style that his eminence grew. His stature within Scottish Protestantism rose and even he began to feel that it was ultimately God who had called him to preach. By June 1547, however, the situation abruptly changed from the Protestants' point of view.

For much of the early sixteenth century, Scotland had been riven by political instability and upheaval.[9] James V had had a long period as king while still a minor and, as had happened in similar circumstances in England in the century before (a period made famous by Shakespeare's history plays on the Wars of the Roses), there had been much aristocratic feuding and factional fighting over who would be the *real* ruler in the King's minority. James, on attaining majority, had decided to remain a loyal Catholic and had compounded this by marrying Mary of Guise, a member of France's most powerful Catholic and strongly anti-Protestant noble family. James in turn had died young, leaving a minority once again. Mary of Guise was the Regent, and was thus staunchly Catholic, pro-French and therefore anti-English. The nominal Queen of Scots, Mary, was therefore raised Catholic and was eventually married to the young French heir, Francis, of the zealously Catholic Valois dynasty. (Mary, born in 1542, was in France from 1547 until 1561.) Political mutability was therefore almost guaranteed again, and this is precisely what happened. Mary of Guise had persuaded her French compatriots to send an army, by sea, to crush the Protestant rebellion. The St. Andrews garrison was bombarded and forced to surrender. The peaceful (and not unfavourable) surrender terms were swiftly reneged upon. John Knox was taken into French custody and was turned into a galley slave in the French fleet.

This was a terrible period in Knox's life. It took nineteen dreadful months of physical suffering before he was released, at the instigation of the English government. On the one hand, Knox's faith emerged deeper from the experience. On the other, his physical health never truly recovered.[10]

In England
As we have seen from the Cranmer chapter, England was now under a *doctrinally* strong Protestant government for the first time.[11] It was still unsafe for Knox to return to Scotland, which was still under pro-French Catholic rule.

(One of the problems, politically, for the Reformers, was that since the English naturally supported the pro-English Protestant party, Protestants in Scotland were inevitably associated with Scotland's historic national enemy, England, and Catholics with her equally historic national ally – the 'Auld Alliance' – France. In England and Germany, by contrast, Protestantism was increasingly seen by many as the patriotic option, supporting the national faith as opposed to the faith of an alien foreign power. Since Scottish Protestantism eventually worked out in a different way from England's – a non-episcopal, Presbyterian form instead of the Anglican system – Scottish Protestants were eventually able to be good patriots and firm Protestants at the same time. But that stage was not reached in Knox's lifetime.) Consequently Knox found himself a preacher in Protestant England. But he managed to get an appointment as near to Scotland as possible, in the garrison town of Berwick, situated right on the still semi-hostile border with Scotland. He was away from home, but as close as he could safely get.

In 1551 he received a new appointment in Newcastle, further south but still not too far away from Scotland. He was also promoted, by being created one of the six new Royal Chaplains to the young King Edward VI. He was now expected to engage in itinerant preaching and evangelism, to ensure the Protestantism of the English church. (As we saw from the chapter on Cranmer, Eamon Duffy, in his seminal work, *The Stripping of the Altars*, has shown fairly conclusively that except in some areas, English Protestantism was only skin deep.[12] If this is indeed the case, as Duffy seems to demonstrate, Knox would probably have been well aware of this and would naturally have wanted to remedy the situation through his preaching.)

Knox was also expected to preach at Court.[13] He was consequently offered the Bishopric of Rochester, then one of the most important sees in the Church of England (and one which has been held by Evangelicals in recent years of the nineteenth century as well). Knox refused the appointment, and also that of Vicar of All Hallows Church in London, a key parish with much influence. However, although his formal influence was not great as a result of his rejections, his informal influence was very profound.

His itinerant preaching ministry took him all over what are called the 'Home Counties', the prosperous regions in the south of England around London. Not only did he preach in the capital, but in Buckinghamshire and also in Kent, the county nearest to France and one in which Protestantism had traditionally been strong. (During the time of the Marian persecution of 1553-1558 a disproportionately large number of Protestant martyrs came from the areas in which Knox had preached.)

Knox also had much behind the scenes influence on the evolving Prayer Book, details of which we saw in the chapter on Cranmer. Knox advised on the new *42 Articles* for the 1552 Prayer Book, and was among those successful in lobbying for the so-called 'Black Rubric' in the Communion Service.[14] This denied the literal presence of Christ in the bread and wine – taking it, as we have seen, closer to Zwingli's position[15] – and also made it clear that kneeling before the elements did not, as in the Catholic church, imply any kind of adoration of the bread and wine itself.

In exile

As we saw, Mary Tudor's accession to the throne in 1553 meant an end to the great Protestant experiment of Edward VI. Once again Knox found himself obliged to flee for safety. Since his native Scotland was still unsafe, he was now forced to flee to Continental Europe, where he had wanted to escape in the first place back in 1546.

The fact that he was once again a fugitive, this time further away from Scotland than before, caused Knox to turn his mind to politics, and to the relationship between a faithful Christian and his or her political overlords.

As we saw in the Luther chapter, the formula *cuius regio eius religio* (whose region or country, his religion) enabled rulers to decide between Protestantism and Catholicism on behalf of their subjects.[16] Germany itself – more properly, the Holy Roman Empire – was a patchwork of comparatively small sovereign entities. This meant, therefore, that a Catholic in Saxony or Hesse, or a Protestant in Bavaria or Bohemia, did not have to go far to find fellow Germans of like persuasion. However, England and Scotland were far bigger political entities. Furthermore, unlike much of continental Europe, each had been a *united* political entity for centuries. (Even France was not as it is today until the eighteenth century, though the major foreign ruler, England, had effectively been expelled in the century preceding Knox.) As a result, there was no Protestant part of England where Protestantism was tolerated or lawful. Mary's accession as a devout Catholic meant that *all* of England was now out of bounds to Protestant believers.

Hitherto Protestants, like their Catholic equivalents, had been very loyal to their secular rulers. Calvin and Zwingli had been invited to cities where the rulers had turned

Protestant, Cranmer worked closely with Henry VIII in establishing English Protestantism, and Luther could not have done what he did without either the protection or direct connivance of Protestant princes in Germany.

To Knox, though, it seemed very clear that one ruler, Mary of Guise, was preventing the establishment of biblical Reformed faith in Scotland. In England, one person's accession to the throne, Mary Tudor, in place of her half-brother Edward VI, was turning the country from a godly Protestant one into one that was reverting to Roman Catholicism and actually persecuting the very same Protestants who had been providing vital spiritual leadership only a very short while before. In other words, Knox realised that getting Reformation was as much a political process as it was a spiritual matter.

The key question therefore inevitably arose, one that had not really been asked effectively by the other four subjects of this book: was it lawful to overthrow an unrighteous sovereign, someone whose existence on the throne meant that the establishment of biblical, Protestant and Reformed Christianity was impossible?[17]

Knox's realisation that resistance might be necessary thus marks him out as radical in a way that the others had rejected. Even Calvin, a political and spiritual exile from his native France, had not advocated that lawful rulers could legitimately be overthrown.[18] To Knox, now a double exile both from Scotland and England, there did not seem to be any alternative if Protestant Christianity was to be established in Britain.

However, his first attempt to encourage resistance, his *Faithful Admonition*, was not a great success.[19] Written in 1554 to encourage those English Protestants left behind under Mary's rule, it was written in what many have felt to be rather severe language. It alienated many of those whom it was designed to help, especially since they felt it was very easy for someone who had fled abroad to write so vehemently while leaving those stuck behind under an unsympathetic regime to face the consequences.[20]

Knox's ideal port of call was Geneva, which he regarded as only a little less than heaven on earth: a truly Christian, reformed democracy. His great hero, Calvin, ordered him instead to go to minister to a congregation of English exiles based in the Imperial German Free City of Frankfurt. There, though, Knox soon found himself enmeshed in the politics of English exiles.[21] Disputes rose among them, and like many exiled groups before and since, they ended up falling out rather vehemently amongst themselves.[22] Knox's ministry proved a casualty, and he found himself back in Geneva, where he remained, to his enormous joy and delight, until 1559 (with the occasional clandestine visit to England and Scotland).[23] He married Marjory Bowes, whom he had met while living in Berwick, and enjoyed a few years of domestic bliss.[24]

He kept in touch with Scotland, whose changing circumstances he followed very closely. To the Scottish nobles of Protestant sympathies, he advocated the cause of 'justifiable resistance' to Catholic rule.[25] In his *Letter of Wholesome Counsel*, written in 1556, he urged Protestants to hold weekly meetings, despite the legal restrictions placed against them, and he was overjoyed at hearing feedback on how fast such meetings were growing.[26]

It was while still in exile that Knox wrote a work for which he has become notorious: his *First Blast of the Trumpet Against The Monstrous Regiment of Women*.[27]

This book has given Knox the reputation of a dour
misogynist. While it is probably true to say that Knox had
reservations about female rulers, the work is, in fact, far
more of a political work than an anti-female diatribe.[28] He
was essentially denouncing three contemporary women
rulers: Mary of Guise in Scotland, Mary Tudor in England
and Mary of Medici in France – all of whom were using
their power to suppress Protestant freedom in their
respective domains. Although it can be accused of being
somewhat intemperate in tone, it is principally a work
against tyranny and in favour of granting freedom to
oppressed Protestants.

Knox's misfortune was that by the time it was finally
published, Mary Tudor was dead and her Protestant half-
sister Elizabeth was on the English throne. Needless to say,
though a Protestant herself, Elizabeth did not appreciate
either its tone or the fact that it was disrespectful to
legitimate rulers, even if they were of Catholic faith.
Therefore, the door back to England, which opened with
Elizabeth's accession in 1558 and the restoration of
Protestant rule, did not open for Knox.

However in 1559, after an effective absence of twelve
years, Knox was once more back in Scotland.

Returns to Scotland
The situation there was still highly dangerous for Protes-
tants. In 1559, in the treaty of Cateau-Cambresis, France
(Scotland's ally) and Spain (England's ally) made peace.[29]
Mary of Guise, still regent for her daughter Mary over in
France, decided that peace gave her a perfect opportunity
to suppress Protestantism. She therefore ordered Protes-
tant preachers to assemble before her on May 10th.

Their response was twofold: one spiritual and one political. Spiritually, they felt that they needed Knox back with them. They summoned him from Geneva and, despite the fact that all the earlier risks still existed, he decided to accept their call. His years of exile were over. Politically, their response was to form a fully-armed mass movement of Protestants of all classes, aristocratic and poor alike. Called the Congregation, the nobles in charge of it, the Lords of the Congregation, summoned and assembled a military force in self-defence.

Events moved rapidly.[30] Knox joined them on May 4th and preached a great rallying sermon which strengthened their morale. By June, the Congregation's forces had managed to take Edinburgh, the capital itself. Knox, however, was realistic enough to know that this was temporary. In France, King Henry II had died and his feeble-minded son, Francis, Mary Queen of Scot's husband, was on the throne as King. The Guise family were now the power behind both the French and Scottish thrones, and that was bound to be a major threat to the militarily far weaker forces of the Scottish Protestant Congregation.

The situation was grave. Mary Stuart was the Catholic claimant to the English throne, since Catholics regarded Elizabeth Tudor as being illegitimate. If the Guises were truly successful, they would be able to claim England, Scotland and France, through the half-Guise, Mary Queen of Scots. The English were fully aware of the dangers, but were not in much of a position to do anything to help. They did, though, understand the *political* as well as spiritual consequences for England of an outright Catholic victory for the Guise faction in Scotland. (Once more the political was the spiritual, as so often in Reformation times.)

Consequently, as McEwen has pointed out, 'only Knox's superhuman exertions and indomitable spirit kept the cause in being'.[31] Elizabeth was not happy with what she perceived to be Knox's misogyny, following the notorious *First Blast*. But Scottish Protestantism, and its political victory, proved to be an essential part of England's national line of defence. Therefore, in 1560, 10,000 English troops were sent to aid the Scottish Protestants. At the same time, the Catholic and Guise champion in Scotland, Mary of Guise herself, died. The Catholic cause now had a serious setback. The French troops withdrew, and the Protestant triumph appeared complete.

Knox's great moment sadly proved illusory. As in England, the desire of the aristocracy for land meant that the nobility kept the land that they sequestered from the Church. This was to have a very major financial impact on Knox's dreams for a new Calvinistic Scottish church.

Knox and other reformers placed the *First Book of Discipline*[32] before the Scottish Parliament. He laid out proposals about how to finance the new organisation, which depended on the massive pre-Reformation endowment income being maintained. For worship there was to be a *Book of Common Order* (popularly known as *Knox's liturgy*). Elders were to be elected annually by the people, and the elders were to help ministers with discipline. Ministers were to be popularly elected, but only after their doctrine and lifestyle were thoroughly approved first by other ministers. The best ministers were to become area superintendents of areas based on the former ecclesiastical boundaries, and were to be helped by provincial synods of ministers and elders.

The *Book of Discipline* also gave very rigorous

educational criteria for leadership in the new church, and it took very seriously the church's traditional commitment to care for the poor.[33]

All this was highly commendable in an ideal world. But Knox did not take into account the powerful vested interests of a Scottish noble class who looked forward to profiting from newly acquired church lands – as their English equivalents had done. As in England, this had the political advantage of giving the most influential political group a literal stake in maintaining the Reformation – not even Mary Tudor had been able to reverse the dissolution of the monasteries. But it also meant that the new church, unlike its Catholic predecessor, did not have any degree of substantial independent income. Consequently, what was referred to as Knox's 'devout imaginings' were defeated.[34] He would have a doctrinally resolute Protestant church, but with nothing like the position and influence for which he had hoped.

By 1561 Knox's *annus mirabilis* was over: Mary Queen of Scots returned to her native Scotland, her mentally unstable French husband prematurely dead.

The caricature of Knox in a film such as *Mary Queen of Scots* (starring Vanessa Redgrave) is perhaps unfair. But it is true to say that Mary regarded a preacher as potent and powerful as Knox as a substantial threat. After a few preliminary skirmishes, their fourth encounter was serious. Knox was able to use his influence to scupper a proposed marriage between Mary and the Spanish Prince Don Carlos of Spain. However angry Mary was with him, the Privy Council of Scotland refused to convict him. To add further insult, Knox, whose beloved first wife Marjory had died, married as his second wife Mary's very distant cousin, Margaret

Stewart, daughter of the leading Protestant Lord Ochiltree.

By 1564 Mary had dismissed her Protestant advisers, or, as one writer has laconically stated, she 'undertook the mismanagement of her own affairs'.[35] Plots and counter-plots took place, involving Mary's debauched husband, Henry Lord Darnley, and her more moral and resolutely Protestant illegitimate half-brother, Lord James Stewart, Earl of Moray. Visitors to the Palace of Holyrood are always shown the gruesome spot where Mary's servant Rizzio was murdered in a ghoulish collaboration between Darnley and the Protestant Lords.[36] Knox was not himself involved, though it has been argued that Knox knew ahead of the murder plot and was therefore complicit by his silence before the event.

Not long afterwards Darnley was himself murdered in another plot. Mary's attempt to rely on her new favourite and third husband, the Earl of Bothwell, proved futile. After further mayhem, she was deposed in 1567 in favour of her infant son James VI (later King James I of England from 1603 and the King James of the King James Version of the Bible). The Earl of Moray became Regent, making Scotland safe for Protestantism,[37] until he himself was murdered in 1570 and Scotland was plunged into civil war again.

Knox himself had to flee Edinburgh in 1571, when he found himself on the wrong side of factional political strife.[38] He had had a paralytic stroke, and his effective preaching career was over. He died the next autumn, back in Edinburgh, on November 24, 1572. Scotland remained chaotic for a while to come, but at least the Protestant Reformation was safe. The Church of Scotland remains to this day, along with its many offshoots including the Free Church of Scotland, as his abiding legacy.

References

1. S. Lamont, *The Swordbearer: John Knox and the European Reformation* (London, 1991) pp. 8-9 and 188-189. Some early authors put his birth as 1505, a date now disproved in favour of 1514; see also James S. McEwen, *The Faith of John Knox* (London, 1961) p. 1 and J. Ridley, *John Knox* (Oxford, 1968) pp. 13-14 and pp. 531-534 for a detailed discussion.

2. Cameron, pp. 385-386; Lamont, pp. 1-3 and 95-96; Ridley, pp. 361-385.

3. See McEwen, *The Faith*, pp. 101-105.

4. Lamont, pp. 9-10; Ridley, pp. 15-18; and McEwen, *The Faith*, pp. 11-23 for an important look at Scottish faith pre-Knox.

5. J. S. McEwen, ed., 'John Knox', *Encyclopaedia Britannica,* Macropaedia, vol. 10, 15th edn. (Chicago, 1975) p. 495; see also Ridley, pp. 16-17.

6. Lamont, pp. 11-12; and McEwen, 'John Knox', p. 495; see also Ridley, pp. 27-44 and McEwen, *The Faith*, p. 101.

7. McEwen, *The Faith*, p. 919; see also Lamont, pp. 32-38.

8. Ridley, pp. 50, 54-66.

9. Lamont, pp. 18-21; Ridley, pp. 1-12 on what a rough, often violent place pre-Reformation Scotland used to be.

10. Ridley, pp. 78-79.

11. See also Ridley, p. 88 and pp. 90-91.

12. Duffy, passim: this is a main theme of the book.

13. Lamont, pp. 60-68 and Ridley, pp. 117-118 and 121-122.

14. Lamont, pp. 61-63; McEwen, *The Faith*, p. 920; Ridley, pp. 106-114.

15. For an analysis of Zwingli's views and Knox, see Ridley, pp. 91-92 and McEwen, *The Faith*, pp. 45-60 for how closely Zwingli and Calvin respectively influenced him.

16. See the relevant pages of the Luther chapter and its footnotes for references.

17. Lamont, pp. 6-7 and 93-95; McEwen, p. 920; Ridley, p. 171 (and a useful comparison with other, often more radical, groups in Europe on pp. 172-174); see also Cameron, pp. 355-356.

18. See Ridley, pp. 178-179 and 529-530.

19. Lamont, pp. 75-77; Ridley, pp. 174-178.

20. Ridley, pp. 185-186.

21. Lamont, pp. 77-82; Ridley, pp. 187-214 for a detailed account.

22. Ridley, p. 188.

23. Lamont, p. 84 and Ridley, p. 215.

24. For a sympathetic treatment of Knox's often maligned attitude to women, see Lamont, pp. 53-59; see also Ridley, pp. 130-144.

25. McEwen, *The Faith*, p. 520; Lamont, p. 88; Ridley, pp. 255, 260-261 and 274-275.

26. Ridley, pp. 255-257.

27. Lamont, pp. 92-96; Ridley, pp. 265-285.

28. Ridley, p. 267.

29. See Ridley, p. 336 for the political implications of this treaty.

30. Lamont, pp. 99-122; for a detailed description of the events, see Ridley, pp. 315-385.

31. McEwen, *The Faith*, pp. 920-921.

32. Ridley, pp. 377-379; Lamont, pp. 119-120; Cameron, p. 385.

33. Lamont, pp. 123-126 on the devastating long-term social effects on Scotland of the failure of Parliament to implement Knox's social and educational vision.

34. McEwen, *The Faith*, p. 3.

35. McEwen, 'John Knox', p. 497

36. His name can be spelled Riccio: see Lamont, pp. 150-153 for the details.

37. Ridley, pp. 476-500.

38. Ibid., pp. 499-500.

Conclusion

With the death of John Knox, we come full circle to the issues that we raised in the Introduction.

What was the Reformation all about? How did it come into being? What were its unifying and dividing features?

We can also ask about the spiritual legacy today of the Reformers selected in this book. Many of the readers will be theological college or seminary students, some will be pastors or church leaders of some kind, and others, maybe that mysterious person dreamed of by publishers' marketing departments, 'the intelligent lay person in the pew'. As we shall see, though, the clergy/laity distinction implied by such a common phrase is, in fact, theologically illegitimate if one takes the theology of the Reformation seriously.

Perhaps you would like to refresh yourself at this point by rereading the overview of the Reformation found in the Introduction and at the beginning of the chapter on Luther.

We saw that the Reformation was the beginning of something new: the abolition of the old sacramental structure of the church and the rediscovery of living the Christian life *sola fidei*, by faith alone. It was this that made Luther so different from people keen to reform from within, such as Contarini and Erasmus. So, while the desire to reform the church was not at all new (Francis of Assisi and others had been trying to do that centuries before), Luther's discovery made the consequences of reform even more dramatic than they had been previously.

This is bolstered by the other Reformation cry of *sola scriptura*: scripture alone is authoritative, and not the tradition of the Church. God speaks to us *directly* through his Word, and the whole mediative role of the late medieval church crumbles.

I therefore agree with those, such as Euan Cameron,[1]

181

who argue that the third basic change, consequent on the first two, is the role of the laity. Here Luther, with his rediscovery of the Petrine doctrine of the priesthood of all believers, leads the way, as does Zwingli with his strong reliance on city councils composed of the laity. Indeed, as John Stott shows in his book *One People*, the distinction between laity and clergy actually vanished if one examined the matter biblically. Luther, Zwingli and others may not have realised the full consequences of the priesthood of all believers in their own lifetimes. However, one can argue legitimately that it became increasingly apparent as time progressed. The very plethora of denominations within Protestantism today is surely proof positive of such a claim. One only has to look at the large number of splits from the original Church of Scotland to illustrate the point.

Sola fidei, *sola scriptura* and the priesthood of all believers were all revolutionary doctrines in the sixteenth century, each one at the heart of the Reformation and of the theology of the five subjects of this book. Nowadays we almost take them for granted and thereby forget how astonishing they would have appeared at the time they were rediscovered.

We also saw how the Reformation came in very different ways, however much we might like to think that it was an overwhelming tide of spiritual hunger sweeping across Europe. Politics played a pivotal role. As I argued earlier, to say this does not diminish in any way the providential role of God: he is, as the books of Exodus, Daniel and Nehemiah all show us, as capable of using secular rulers to bring in his will as he is of using the godly. Pharaoh was no saint, nor was Cyrus, yet God used both of them for his people's benefit. We need not worry therefore if God used the proto-nationalism of the German Imperial Knights or the dynastic desires of King Henry VIII for a male heir to bring about his purposes. Secular historians may feel that the invention of printing in Germany, just before Luther's Reformation began there, was a happy coincidence. Those of us who believe in divine sovereignty might see a different cause! Secular writers could fairly point out that Catholics responding to Luther were soon equally adept at using the new invention for propaganda purposes: a lesson, therefore, to Protestant historians not to wax too lyrical about the providential coincidences of history!

We can therefore look at the different circumstances of each figure.

Luther would seem to be a case of a *spiritual* movement originating Reformation, and being able to survive because of *political* support. One only has to remember the earlier fifteenth-century martyrs to see that Reformation unsupported by politics did not last long. If one looks back to Jan Hus, Bohemia failed to instigate the Reformation despite strong local support from followers such as the Hussites and Utraquists. If one looks forward to the 1620s, we witness the defeat of the Protestant forces at the Battle of the White Mountain outside Prague. The result was that Czech Protestantism was all but wiped out. It then becomes possible to claim that politically unsupported Protestantism was a frail flower which withered when Counter-Reformation forces were able to retaliate. It was especially true when physical force and persecution was used as well as missionary endeavour. Without Frederick the Wise in Saxony, and the support of other Princes subsequently, Luther's fate and that of the Lutherans could have been similar. We forget all too easily, looking at countries as strongly Roman Catholic as Poland or Austria, that they too once had strong Protestant minorities.

In the case of Zwingli, his conversion to Protestantism and the decision of the Council in Zürich to back him, came very close together chronologically. In Calvin's case, Geneva was already Protestant when he came. In both situations, the liberating effect of Protestantism on the laity can be seen clearly.[2] Ordinary people were suddenly empowered to make major theological decisions, something which they had been prevented from doing for centuries. As Zwingli's life shows, though, not all democracies voted for Reformation. But as Calvin's demonstrates, if they did, then the possibilities were endless.

England, and Cranmer, shows that Reformation could come for entirely political reasons. There were certainly plenty of supporters of Luther around, but they have been shown to be very much a minority in England as a whole. It was not until Edward VI that Cranmer was able to get a truly Protestant Church of England, and the vicious counterattack under Mary shows how fragile that was. It was not until the accession of Elizabeth, well over twenty years after the original break with Rome, that England became permanently Protestant. Even then it was held by a thread. If Elizabeth I had been overthrown and Mary Queen of Scots imposed on the English throne, as many wanted, England might have reverted to Catholicism once again. The triumph of the Reformation in England was never a foregone conclusion.

The Catholicism of Mary Stuart naturally brings us to Knox, the only one of the five who argued effectively that it was legitimate to overthrow a sovereign. Wishart's martyrdom shows what could easily have happened to Scottish Protestantism: a fate similar, say, to those in Poland, where many nobles supported Protestantism but were eventually defeated. As in England, Protestantism's eventual success was never inevitable. It was, one could argue, the result of a political *coup d'etat* and the fortuitous death of Mary of Guise. Had the rebellion gone the other way, Knox's fate could have matched that of Wishart. Knox was fortunate to have been condemned to the galleys in an earlier attempt at Reformation, rather than being executed.

Once again, for those of us who, as Protestants, are naturally inclined to favour the Reformation, these narrow escapes are signs of the overruling of God. Lest we be complacent, though, we should remember that those tiny Protestant communities existing in Central Europe (such as in Poland or Austria) would have a very different perspective. Likewise, in Eastern Europe, especially in Orthodox areas such as the Balkans or Russia, the Reformation never really got going at all, particularly in those Orthodox countries under Islamic rule in the Ottoman Empire. In such places persecution against Protestants still exists, as recent changes of the law in Russia demonstrate clearly.

To be fair, Protestants and Catholics continued to persecute each other for two centuries after the Reformation, although such behaviour stopped effectively in most places by the beginning of the nineteenth century. It is worth noting that the decision in the fledgling United States to break the link between Church and State, a bond upon which all five Reformers in this book were in full agreement, has paradoxically created one of the most Christian and actively Protestant countries on earth. This would have astonished the five Reformers for whom the Church-State link remained pivotal.

Similarly, those of the five who encountered the growing Anabaptist movement opposed it, sometimes with great violence. Those who hold today to many of the principles of the so-called 'Radical Reformation' will surely look at the five subjects of this book in a very different light. However I would argue that, despite my own Baptistic and American-style Church-State separation feelings, if Luther and the other early Reformers had *not* got the support of some Princes or City Councils, the Reformation would have faced massive difficulties in getting off the ground. God could, of course, have arranged it otherwise. But since, as in Old Testament times, he chose not to, one can argue that the desire of the five subjects of this book to work in conjunction with State power was beneficial to the Reformation process.

This does not mean, as I mentioned in the introduction, that one has to endorse *all* they did: the bloodthirsty tirades of Luther against peasants and Anabaptists, and the decisions by Zwingli *literally* to fight for the Reformation are surely not things we would support today. (At least, I would hope not!) The five were all men of their time as well as being men of God. Like David or Peter they made mistakes and were often all too human. Protestants believe that *all* Christians are saints. We should not therefore be tempted to make ordinary mortals into special saints with cult-like devotion.

The Reformation also shows, surely, that the Church can survive diversity and disagreement. From disputes written up in the *Book of Acts* through to the Luther-Zwingli Colloquy of Marburg and disagreement over the Eucharist, fellow Christians have differed one from the other. Yet it seems that on all *essential* matters, on the great doctrines of justification by faith alone or the supreme authority of Scripture, our five were in complete agreement, albeit with minor differences of emphasis. I trust this book has shown that Calvin was by no means alone in his support for predestination, and that he was considerably less prone to State violence than Luther, Zwingli and Knox. Protestantism may have its divisions, but it has also had considerable growth.

The growth of Protestantism, well beyond the countries of Europe to the global faith that it is today, brings us naturally to the pastoral side of the conclusion and those present-day lessons that may not have been implicit in what I have written so far. Protestants claim the Reformation, but how truly faithful to its principles are we?

As we have just seen, Protestants often criticise the Catholic 'Cult of Saints'. But how often do we unwittingly do something similar? Many Protestant traditions, including Presbyterians of most hues, look back in awe and gratitude to Calvin. There are churches named Lutheran to this day. Other denominations are no different, whether it is the Wesley brothers, Smyth and Helwys, Azusa Street or whatever your past hero's name or location might be. We all too easily tend to look at Scripture through the prism of *their* teaching rather than, as the Reformers did, looking *directly* to scripture itself, as the doctrine of *sola scriptura* surely teaches. It would be too ironic if, by quoting, say, Calvin or Luther slavishly, we treat them as being infallible! If we teach that the Pope is not infallible, then neither is any other church leader, however revered.

Similarly, how much do we look to the pastor (or vicar

or elder or whatever we call him) to do everything for us? Do we examine Scripture for ourselves, weigh up the Sunday sermon in the light of the Bible (as Paul instructed us to do), or simply take it from the minister? Do we develop ourselves spiritually, seeking to grow and mature together actively with the other believers in the Church, through our conversations, our reading, our home groups? Or are we completely passive? We can hardly condemn the clerical-led nature of Roman Catholicism when we ourselves are the spiritual equivalent of couch potatoes! Roman Catholicism itself has changed much, not least in the encouragement of lay activity. All the more reason for professing Protestants to be active likewise.

Finally, as Billy Graham once said, 'You may be a deacon in your church and not be born again.' The Reformation doctrine of *sola fidei*, justification by faith alone, is a lynchpin of the Protestant understanding of Christian faith, and thus, for the Protestant, of Christianity itself. It is thus the ultimate guard against complacency. If we are not saved by works but by faith, as a gift of the grace of God, then none of us has any cause to regard ourselves as a Christian by virtue of our parentage, our country of birth, our contributions to church funds, or any other outward marker. It is by grace we are saved through faith, and by faith alone. Our social standing, our heritage, our denomination: all make no difference whatsoever to our standing before God.

As church membership becomes or remains respectable, we must always be challenged to our core as to our true faith before God. It is on our relationship with him, directly and individually, that we stand or fall, whatever position or rank in a church that we may or may not hold. *Sola fidei* was the great turning point and rallying call of the Reformation and of the five subjects of this book. If we are to be true to them we must be true to the biblical faith which they proclaimed. They – and their Saviour – would expect no less.

References

1. I would argue more explicitly than he does on this point.

2. As referred to often in this book and throughout Euan Cameron's history.

Bibliography

Ackroyd, Peter. *Life of Thomas More* (London, 1998).

Anderson, Benedict. *Imagined Communities,* 2nd edn. (London and New York, 1991).

Atkinson, James. 'Reform' in *The Lion/Eerdmans Handbook to the History of Christianity* (London and Grand Rapids, 1977) pp.360-398.

Bainton, Roland H. *Here I Stand* (Nashville and London, 1955).

_____. *The Reformation of the Sixteenth Century*, 2nd revised edn. (Boston, 1985).

Barclay, Oliver R. *Evangelicalism in Britain 1935-1995: A Personal Sketch* (Leicester, 1997).

Betts, R. R. 'Constitutional Development and Political Thought in Western Europe' in G. R. Elton, ed. *The New Cambridge Modern History*, Vol. 2 (Cambridge, 1958) pp. 464-477.

Bromiley, G. W. 'Zwingli', *Encyclopaedia Britannica,* Macropaedia, vol. 30, 15th edn. (Chicago, 1975) pp. 1178-1180.

Cameron, Euan. *History of the European Reformation* (Oxford, 1991).

Catherwood, Christopher. *A Crash Course on Church History* (London, 1998).

_____. 'Nationalism, Academia and Modernity: a Reply', *Transformation*, vol. 14, no. 4, October/December 1997, pp. 26-31.

_____. *Why the Nations Rage* (London, 1997).

Chadwick, Owen. *The Reformation* (London, 1964).

Cross, F.L. ed. 'Richard Baxter', *The Oxford Dictionary of the Christian Church* (Oxford and New York, 1957) p. 143.

Dickens, A. G. *The English Reformation* (London, 1965).

Dowey, E. A. 'John Calvin', *Encyclopaedia Britannica*, vol. 4, 14th edn., rev. (Chicago, 1970), pp. 671-674.

Duffy, Eamon. *The Stripping of the Altars* (London and New Haven, 1992).

Ebeling, Gerhard. *Luther: An Introduction to His Thought* (London, 1972).

Elton, G. R. 'Constitutional Development in Germany' in *The New Cambridge Modern History*, Vol. 2 (Cambridge, 1958) pp. 477-480.

_____. *England under the Tudors* (Cambridge, 1953).

_____. 'Thomas Cranmer', in *Encyclopaedia Britannica*, Macropaedia, vol. 3, 15th edn., rev. (Chicago, 1990), p. 713-715.

_____. 'The Reformation in England', in *The New Cambridge Modern History*, Vol. 2 (Cambridge, 1958) pp. 226-250.

Febure, Lucien and Henri-Jean Martin. *The Coming of the Book* (London, 1976, English translation; French original, *L'Apparition du Livre*, Paris, 1958).

Fernandez-Armesto, Felipe and Derek Wilson. *Reformation: Christianity and the World 1500-2000* (London and New York, 1996).

George, Timothy. *The Theology of the Reformers* (Nashville, 1988).

Giddens, Anthony. *Politics and Sociology in the Thought of Max Weber* (London, 1972).

Habsburg, Otto von. *Charles V* (London, 1970, English translation; French original, Paris, 1967).

Hastings, Adrian. *The Construction of Nationhood: Ethnicity, Religion and Nationalism* (Cambridge, 1997).

Hillerbrand, Hans J. *The World of the Reformation* (London, 1973).

Johnson, Pamela and Bob Scribner. *The Reformation in Germany and Switzerland* (Cambridge and New York, 1993).

Kennedy, Paul. *The Rise and Fall of the Great Powers* (London and New York, 1987).

Kingdon, R. M. 'John Calvin' in *Encyclopaedia Britannica*, Macropaedia, vol. 3, 15th edn. (Chicago, 1975) pp. 671-675.

Lamont, S. *The Swordbearer: John Knox and the European Reformation* (London, 1991).

Lane, Tony. 'A Flood of Bibles' in *The Lion/Eerdmans Handbook to the History of Christianity* (London and Grand Rapids, 1977) pp. 366-372.

Marsden, George. *The Soul of the American University* (New York and Oxford, 1994).

Mitzman, Arthur. 'Max Weber (1864-1920)' in *Encyclopaedia Britannica*, Macropaedia, vol. 19, 15th edn. (Chicago, 1975) pp. 714-717.

MacCulloch, Diarmaid. *Thomas Cranmer* (London and New Haven, 1996).

McEwen, James S. *The Faith of John Knox* (London, 1961).

_____. 'John Knox', *Encyclopaedia Britannica*, Micropaedia, vol. vi, 15th edn., rev. (Chicago, 1986), p. 919-921.

McGrath, Alister. *A Cloud of Witnesses* (Leicester, 1990).

_____. *Intellectual Origins of the European Reformation* (Oxford, 1987).

_____. *A Life of John Calvin: A Study in the Shaping of Western Culture* (Oxford, 1990).

_____. *Luther's Theology of the Cross* (Oxford, 1985).

McManners, J. ed. T*he Oxford Illustrated History of Christianity* (Oxford and New York, 1990).

McNair, Philip. 'Seeds of Renewal' in *The Lion/Eerdmans Handbook to the History of Christianity* (London and Grand Rapids, 1977) pp. 346-359.

Packer, James I. *Evangelism and the Sovereignty of God* (London and Chicago, 1961).

_____. 'The Faith of the Protestants', in *The Lion/Eerdmans Handbook to the History of Christianity* (London and Grand Rapids, 1977) pp. 374-375.

Payne, Ernest. 'The Anabaptists', in G. R. Elton, ed., *The New Cambridge Modern History*, vol. 2 (Cambridge, 1958) pp. 119-133.

Porter, H. C., ed. *Erasmus and Cambridge*, translator, D. F. S. Thomson (Toronto, 1963).

Ridley, J. *John Knox* (Oxford, 1968).

Rosenberg, Hans. 'Pope Innocent III' in *The Lion/Eerdmans Handbook to the History of Christianity* (London and Grand Rapids, 1977) p.255.

Rupp, E. G. 'Martin Luther' in *Encyclopaedia Britannica*, Macropaedia, vol. 11, 15th edn., (Chicago, 1975), pp. 188-196.

_____. 'The Reformation in Zurich, Strassburg (sic) and Geneva' in G. R. Elton, ed., *The New Cambridge Modern History*, vol. 2 (Cambridge, 1958) pp. 96-119.

[Author unknown], 'Servetus', *Encyclopaedia Britannica*, Micropaedia, vol. ix, 15th edn. (Chicago, 1975) p. 75.

Spooner, F. C. 'The Habsburg-Valois Struggle', in *The New Cambridge Modern History*, vol. 2 (Cambridge, 1958), pp. 334-358.

Starkey, David. *The Reign of Henry VIII* (London, 1991 edn.).

Stephens, W. P. *Zwingli: An Introduction to His Thought* (Oxford, 1992/4).

Stupperich, R. 'Martin Luther', in *The Lion/Eerdmans Handbook to the History of Christianity* (London, and Grand Rapids, 1977) pp. 362-363.

Index

60 Great Founders
Geoffrey Hanks

ISBN 1 85792 1402   *large format 496 pages*

This book details the Christian origins of 60 organizations, most of which are still committed to the God-given, world-changing vision with which they began. Among them are several mission organizations.

70 Great Christians
Geoffrey Hanks

ISBN 1 871 676 800   *large format 352 pages*

The author surveys the growth of Christianity throughout the world through the lives of prominent individuals who were dedicated to spreading the faith. Two sections of his book are concerned with mission; one section looks at the nineteenth century missionary movement, and the other details mission growth throughout the twentieth century.

Mission of Discovery

ISBN 1 85792 2581   *large format 448 pages*

The fascinating journal of Robert Murray McCheyne's and Andrew Bonar's journeys throughout Palestine and Europe in the 1840s to investigate if the Church of Scotland should set up a mission to evangelise the Jewish people. From their investigation, much modern Jewish evangelism has developed.

Books by **R. C. Sproul**

A Walk With Jesus

376 pages   ISBN 1 85792 260 3 large hardback
A study of the life of Christ, based on the
Gospel of Luke, divided into 104 sections.

Mighty Christ

144 pages   ISBN 1 85792 148 8   paperback
A study of the person and work of Jesus.

The Mystery of the Holy Spirit

192 pages   ISBN 1 871676 63 0   paperback
Examines the role of the Spirit in creation,
salvation and in strengthening the believer.

Ephesians

160 pages   ISBN 1 85792 078 3   paperback
Focus on the Bible Commentary, useful for
devotional study of this important New Testament book.

The Gospel of God

256 pages   ISBN 1 85792 077 5   large hardback
An exposition of the Book of Romans

MENTOR TITLES

Creation and Change
Douglas Kelly
(large format, 272 pages)
A scholarly defence of the literal seven-day account of the creation of all things as detailed in Genesis 1. The author is Professor of Systematic Theology in Reformed Theological Seminary in Charlotte, North Carolina, USA.

The Healing Promise
Richard Mayhue
(large format, 288 pages)
A clear biblical examination of the claims of Health and Wealth preachers. The author is Dean of The Master's Seminary, Los Angeles, California.

Puritan Profiles
William Barker
(hardback, 320 pages)
The author is Professor of Church History at Westminster Theological Seminary, Philadelphia, USA. In this book he gives biographical profiles of 54 leading Puritans, most of whom were involved in the framing of the Westminster Confession of Faith.

Creeds, Councils and Christ
Gerald Bray
(large format, 224 pages)
The author, who teaches at Samford University, Birmingham, Alabama, explains the historical circumstances and doctrinal differences that caused the early church to frame its creeds. He argues that a proper appreciation of the creeds will help the confused church of today.

Christian Focus titles by
Donald Macleod

A Faith to Live By

In this book the author examines the doctrines detailed in the Westminster Confession of Faith and applies them to the contemporary situation facing the church.

ISBN 1 85792 428 2   *Hardback*   *320 pages*

Behold Your God

A major work on the doctrine of God, covering his power, anger, righteousness, name and being. This book will educate and stimulate deeper thinking and worship.

ISBN 1 876 676 509   *paperback*   256 pages

Rome and Canterbury

This book assesses the attempts for unity between the Anglican and Roman Catholic churches, examining the argument of history, the place of Scripture, and the obstacle of the ordination of women.

ISBN 0 906 731 887   *paperback*   *64 pages*

The Spirit of Promise

This book gives advice on discovering our spiritual role in the local church, the Spirit's work in guidance, and discusses various interpretations of the baptism of the Spirit.

ISBN 0 906 731 448   *paperback*   *112 pages*

Shared Life

The author examines what the Bible teaches concerning the Trinity, then explores various historical and theological interpretations regarding the Trinity, before indicating where some of the modern cults err in their views of the Trinity.

ISBN 1-85792-128-3   *paperback*   *128 pages*